# The Executive Guide
# to Strategic Planning

*Patrick J. Below*

*George L. Morrisey*

*Betty L. Acomb*

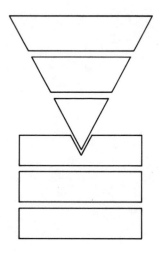

# The Executive Guide
# to Strategic Planning

 Jossey-Bass Publishers

San Francisco   •   Oxford   •   1990

THE EXECUTIVE GUIDE TO STRATEGIC PLANNING
by Patrick J. Below, George L. Morrisey, Betty L. Acomb

Copyright © 1987 by: Jossey-Bass Inc., Publishers
350 Sansome Street
San Francisco, California 94104
&
Jossey-Bass Limited
Headington Hill Hall
Oxford OX3 0BW

Patrick J. Below
George L. Morrisey
Betty L. Acomb

**Library of Congress Cataloging-in-Publication Data**

Below, Patrick J.
  The executive guide to strategic planning.

  (The Jossey-Bass management series)
  Bibliography: p. 127
  Includes index.
  1. Strategic planning.  I. Morrisey, George L.
II. Acomb, Betty L.  III. Title.  IV. Series.
HD30.28.B45  1987      658.4'012      86-27863
ISBN 1-55542-032-X

Manufactured in the United States of America

The paper in this book meets the guidelines for
permanence and durability of the Committee on
Production Guidelines for Book Longevity of the
Council on Library Resources.

JACKET DESIGN BY WILLI BAUM

FIRST EDITION
  *First printing: February 1987*
  *Second printing: January 1988*
  *Third printing: August 1988*
  *Fourth printing: April 1989*
  *Fifth printing: November 1989*
  *Sixth printing: September 1990*
Code 8704

The Jossey-Bass

Management Series

# Contents

What Is a Strategic Plan? • What Is the Integrated Planning Process? • How Does the Strategic Plan Fit into the Integrated Planning Process? • What Are the Elements of the Strategic Plan, and How Do They Fit Together? • What Is the Most Effective Approach to Developing a Strategic Plan? • In Summary

Why Is Commitment Necessary? • Where Does Commitment Start? • What Keeps Individual Managers from Being Committed to Strategic Planning? • What Can Top Management Do to Encourage Total Organization Commitment to Strategic Planning? • What Are the Key Roles of the Planning Team? • In Summary

# Tables and Figures

# Preface

Strategic planning offers a beacon of hope to organizations of all sizes as they search for new methods of long-term management. This book is designed to help operating executives and managers develop practical and realistic strategic plans. Critical questions this book addresses include: What is a strategic plan? What is the process for creating a strategic plan? How is such a plan developed within an organization?

Strategic planning is undergoing a transition characterized by two rapidly emerging trends. The first can be discerned in large corporations that have relied heavily on their corporate planning departments to develop comprehensive strategic plans. Frequently, such plans have not been fully implemented. As a result, there is now a substantial shift of this responsibility from corporate planning departments to operating executives and managers.

The second trend can be seen in small and medium-sized organizations that previously may not have been involved in formal strategic planning. Many are now seeing the need for longer term direction and clarity.

These two trends, originating from distinctly different environments, have converged at the same point: organizations of all sizes are recognizing the need to plan and manage so that both long-term and short-term results can be achieved on a consistent basis. It is our conviction that an Integrated Planning Process, whereby operating executives and managers think strategically and act operationally, is a necessity if organizations are to survive and prosper.

Regardless of an organization's size or experience, there are two key ingredients to making strategic planning work. First, a viable planning process that all managers understand and use is essential. Second, there must be organizational commitment to both the plan and the planning process. A premise of this book is that the process of planning is as important as the plan itself.

### For Whom Is This Book Written and How Can It Be Used?

This book on strategic planning is primarily designed as a guide for chief executive officers (CEOs) and senior executive teams in both the private and public sectors. The CEO and the senior executive team may be at the corporate level or in any major organizational segment, such as a division or department, where there is substantial autonomy.

With that perspective in mind, this book also has particular value for the following:

1. *Executive team members*—for carrying out their own strategic planning efforts
2. *External or internal consultants*—for use as the planning team's guide to developing and implementing a strategic plan
3. *Senior executives*—for individual study and application
4. *Other managers*—for application in their own operations
5. *Management seminar or class instructors*—as a primary, supplementary, or reference text for classes in strategic planning or management

6. *Prospective managers*—as preparation for future responsibilities.

## Why Was This Book Written?

While there are a number of books on strategic planning available, many of them tend to focus on specific analytical techniques. No other book that we are aware of shows a direct tie-in with operational planning and corporate performance and control (or results management)—which constitute what we refer to as an Integrated Planning Process. Based on our experience in working with a wide variety of organizations in both the public and private sectors, the approach we have developed here is straightforward, easy to follow, and written in language that busy executives can grasp quickly and apply. Furthermore, while this book stands alone as a clear guide to the whys and hows of strategic planning, it is designed as part of a three-volume series that will address the total planning effort for an organization, stressing the importance of planning as an ongoing process rather than an annual event. The second book in the series will cover the process of operational planning. The third book will delineate the process of achieving corporate performance and control (or results management), which ensures the execution of the plans.

## Overview of the Contents

The chapters in the book flow logically in line with the normal development of a strategic plan. Chapter One discusses what strategic planning is, its place in the Integrated Planning Process, and the definitions of each of the seven elements of a strategic plan, explaining how they fit together. Chapter Two is concerned with getting organizational commitment to strategic planning; it describes some typical barriers and how they may be overcome. It also defines specifically the individual roles of planning team members.

The next seven chapters describe in detail each of the seven elements of a strategic plan in the sequence in which they normally occur. Chapter Three describes specifically how to develop an organizational mission statement that has the full commitment of the planning team. Chapter Four describes what is involved in strategic analysis, how it should be approached, and what the specific results of strategic analysis should be. Chapter Five provides a methodology for determining an organization's future strategy or direction, including the establishment of priorities. These three chapters are primarily concerned with the strategic thinking part of the strategic planning process.

Chapter Six, which starts the long-range planning part of the process, shows how to select and validate long-term objectives that describe what the organization wishes to have or become at some point in the future. Chapter Seven begins to form the bridge with the operational plan, explaining how to determine cross-functional action plans, described as integrated programs. Chapter Eight provides the means for presenting the financial data generated in earlier steps, putting them into a series of financial projections.

Chapter Nine describes a critical, but often overlooked, part of the strategic plan known as the executive summary. In it, the CEO has the opportunity to pull portions of the plan together with his or her own personal interpretation. Chapter Ten provides a practical summary of strategic plan development and implementation from start to finish. It gets into the frequency of team meetings, executive time required, how and when specific planning efforts are to be completed, and how to ensure that the plan is both understood and implemented throughout the organization. In addition, there are further resources describing four specific strategic analysis techniques and how they can be used within the plan's context. There is also an annotated bibliography describing some of the other works in the field that have influenced the development of this book.

## How Did This Book Come About?

In the mid 1970s, Patrick Below and George Morrisey met at a conference of what was then known as the International MBO Institute. Over the next several years, they met on frequent occasions to discuss the complementary work that each was doing in the area of planning. In 1983, Below and Morrisey met with Betty Acomb to initiate efforts that led to the formation of the Planning Process Group, a nationwide network of consultants who provide planning process consulting services to their clients. Another purpose of this group is to advance the state of the art in management planning by using the method known as the Integrated Planning Process. With the support of this consultant network, organizations of all sizes are using this process to achieve significant results.

The Integrated Planning Process has been developed by Patrick Below in his domestic and international consulting work with a wide variety of client organizations over the past ten years. It is a highly simplified yet comprehensive management process that incorporates George Morrisey's approach to operational planning. The Integrated Planning Process is the foundation on which this three-book series is based.

Through a number of years of working with organizations that were attempting to influence their future through better planning, we have learned that the development or upgrading of a strategic plan is an important undertaking that requires a significant commitment from operating executives. Our intent is to clarify and simplify this task for our readers. Through this book, we hope to function as coach/facilitator as we guide you and your team through the process of developing a strategic plan.

## Acknowledgments

Our thanks go to the many executives in the client organizations we have served, in both the private and public sectors, who have helped us refine the Integrated Planning Process. Any executive team with a strong philosophy and commitment to really involve their people in the planning process can make this strategic planning approach work for them.

We are particularly grateful to the Planning Process Group charter members—Michael Cast, Frederic Clark, William Guthrie, Marie J. Kane, and Robert Zahrowski—for their contributions to the development of the process as well as their feedback on the initial manuscript. Michael and Marie, in particular, made important contributions through their participation in client efforts where the approaches in this book were effectively used.

We also thank George Odiorne for his many contributions to seminal thinking in both planning and management as well as his generosity in sharing openly many valuable ideas and recommendations during the preparation of this book. We extend special recognition to Walter Schaffir for his significant contributions to the strategic planning field, including the importance of the planning coach/facilitator role.

In addition, our grateful appreciation goes to Tim Rinker for his stimulating and creative designs for the graphic illustrations in the book; to Joseph Ferrell for his design of the Planning Process Group logo; and to Ruth Chaney and Betty Stubbs for their cheerful and competent translation of frequently undecipherable material into a well-prepared manuscript.

*November 1986*                   Patrick J. Below
                                  *Appleton, Wisconsin*

                                  George L. Morrisey
                                  *Buena Park, California*

                                  Betty L. Acomb
                                  *Appleton, Wisconsin*

# The Authors

*Patrick J. Below* is president of Patrick J. Below Associates (Appleton, Wisconsin), a management consulting firm founded in 1970. His firm specializes in working with chief executive officers of small and medium-size companies in strategic and operational planning. He is also one of the three principals in the Planning Process Group, a national firm of business planning consultants. He received his B.E.E. degree (1962) from Marquette University and his M.B.A. degree (1967) from Indiana University.

Below's management experience includes eight years in the areas of manufacturing, sales and marketing, and computer systems with General Electric Company and American Can Company. He has also spent ten years as an international business consultant working with companies based in Trinidad.

*George L. Morrisey* is chairman of the Morrisey Group, a management consulting firm, based in Buena Park, California, and a principal in the Planning Process Group, a nationwide consortium of independent planning consultants. He received his B.S. (1951) and M.Ed. (1952) degrees from Springfield (Mass.) College. Morrisey has more than twenty years' experience as a practicing manager and key specialist with such organizations as First Western Bank, Rockwell International, McDonnell Douglas, and the U.S. Postal Service in addition to more than fourteen years as a full-time consultant. He has personally assisted more than 200 business, industrial, service, governmental, and not-for-profit organizations in the areas of strategic and operational planning and results management.

He is the author of twelve books, including *Management by Objectives and Results for Business and Industry, Management by Objectives and Results in the Public Sector, Performance Appraisals for Business and Industry, Performance Appraisals in the Public Sector, Effective Business and Technical Presentations,* and *Getting Your Act Together: Goal Setting for Fun, Health, and Profit* (which complements the popular Salenger Educational Media film with the same title, in which Morrisey is featured in addition to serving as advisor). He is the author and producer of several audio- and video-cassette learning programs, all directed toward helping individuals and organizations become more effective and self-fulfilled.

Morrisey received the Council of Peers Award for Excellence (CPAE), the highest recognition granted to a professional speaker, from the National Speakers Association in 1984 and the national American Society for Training and Development (ASTD) Award for Publications in 1974. He is a member of the boards of directors of the Association for Management Excellence and the National Speakers Association and is on the Advisory Board for the Society for the Advancement of Management (SAM) *Advanced Management Journal.*

*Betty L. Acomb* is a senior partner in Patrick J. Below Associates (Appleton, Wisconsin), a consulting firm specializing in strategic and operational planning. She is also one of the three principals in the Planning Process Group, a national firm of business planning consultants.

Acomb has ten years' experience in public sector management in the areas of strategic and operational planning, program management, community development, and legislative programming. She has served as Director of the Community Contact Program (Cincinnati, Ohio) and Program Manager of Community Action (Rock County, Wisconsin). In addition, she has had extensive experience as a consultant to various public sector groups, including Widowed Persons Service (Richmond, Indiana), Governor's Commission on the Status of Women (Ohio), and Parents of Gifted and Talented Children (Fairfax County, Virginia).

She received her B.A. degree (1973) from Buena Vista College in Iowa and has undertaken postgraduate studies at the University of Wisconsin at Madison.

# The Executive Guide
# to Strategic Planning

# 1

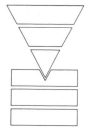

# What Is Strategic Planning?

"If you don't know where you are going, any road will take you there" is a statement attributed to the Koran. Strategic planning determines where your organization should be going so that all organizational efforts can be pointed in that direction. Strategic planning is the single most important function of the CEO (chief executive officer or whoever is designated as the key decision maker), in any organization. That is an awesome responsibility. As a result, the formation of a planning team to assist the CEO in fulfilling this function becomes an absolute necessity. In order for any organization to survive and grow in the future, the CEO and the planning team need to give primary attention to determining what the organization should become.

In order to embark on a successful strategic planning process, the CEO and the planning team need to agree on the following:

1. *Terminology.* The exact meaning and interpretation of terms and concepts must be understood and applied consistently by all who must make the plans work and come alive.
2. *Approach.* There needs to be complete understanding

1

and agreement on the strategic planning approach to be followed. While there are various ways to develop and implement a strategic plan, the approach described here will be practical and straightforward, yet flexible enough to be adapted to your organization's needs.

3. *Separation of strategic from operational planning.* These are two distinctly different thinking and planning processes. Strategic planning requires visionary and directional thinking. Operational planning requires short-term, specific thinking. For example, it would appear that the decision by Sears in the early 1980s to become a total financial network was strategic in nature because it was a marked departure from its former way of doing business. However, the acquisition of companies like Coldwell Banker (real estate) and Dean Witter (securities) logically came as a result of operational decisions triggered by the broader strategic vision.

## What Is a Strategic Plan?

A strategic plan is a framework for carrying out strategic thinking, direction, and action leading to the achievement of consistent and planned results. Seven specific elements comprise this framework:

- organization mission
- strategic analysis
- strategy
- long-term objectives
- integrated programs
- financial projections
- executive summary

Each element is developed and completed individually, but they are all interrelated. Together they form an important management tool for determining the basic nature and concept of an organization, the overall direction or strategy for fulfilling that concept, and a roadmap for carrying out the strategy and achieving long-term results.

The strategic planning process is defined as the on-going involvement of operating executives and managers in producing their organization's strategic plan. A distinctive aspect of this process is its emphasis on team planning. It is this process that builds organizationwide belief and commitment to the strategic plan because the participants have ownership. It is also the process that helps to ensure implementation of the plan.

## What Is the Integrated Planning Process?

The Integrated Planning Process, as developed by Patrick Below, presents a total framework for depicting an organization's planning and control system. Each of the three key words has a specific meaning as we approach the design and implementation of the planning function. Let's examine each individually and then put them all together as we look at the entire process.

*Integrated* means that no part of the planning process can be developed in isolation from the other parts. If planning is to work in any organization, the first step is to clearly identify the various components and determine how they all fit together. Frequently, a strong effort on what is referred to as strategic planning goes to one of two extremes. Either it is a straight-line projection of what the organization has done in the past or it is a lofty picture of some ideal that has little, if any, relationship to what happens either in the annual operating plan or on a day-to-day basis. Furthermore, in many organizations, there is virtually no plan for ensuring that plans are implemented and that the subsequent results are achieved. Each of the three components of the Integrated Planning Process will be addressed in separate volumes. A common thread throughout will be that any truly successful organization will ensure that all portions of the process are completely integrated, both vertically and horizontally. Also, there needs to be a clear understanding throughout the organization as to where it is going and how it is going to get there.

*Planning* incorporates all of the efforts that determine what an organization wants to be, where it is going and how it will get there. Planning is clearly a means and not an end. Plans, in and of themselves, have little value. The purpose of planning is not to produce plans; it is to produce results on a consistent basis. Furthermore, planning must be seen as an ongoing activity, not as an annual event. Consequently, the CEO and the executive team must view planning as a top priority which validates their major decisions and actions.

*Process* suggests that there are distinct skills that must be applied, there is a body of knowledge to be imparted, and there is a sequence of events that must take place. *Process* needs to be distinguished from *procedure*, which is a sequence that must be followed by the numbers. There is a place for procedures in organizational efforts. Planning is *not* a procedure. It is a process that requires a great deal of flexibility and the exercise of good managerial judgment. There will be times when executives may judge that certain portions of the process are not critical to accomplishing the organization's goals. A conscious decision to bypass parts of the process is legitimate. Process, as described here, also requires the active involvement of people in the planning effort. Is there a full understanding of and commitment to planning? Does the process encourage discussion of differing points of view? Does the process promote a feeling of ownership among those involved? Do those affected believe that the planning process is relevant to both their day-to-day efforts and their own future plans?

The Integrated Planning Process is shown in Figure 1.1. It incorporates the three major components—the strategic plan, the operational plan, and results management. It is tied together through the concepts of integration and communication, with a clear recognition that planning is an ongoing people process.

Each of the three components serves a distinctly dif-

Figure 1.1. Integrated Planning Process.

ferent purpose. The strategic plan focuses on the basic nature (mission) and direction (strategy) of the organization.
The operational plan concentrates on how to implement
the strategic plan and produce short-term results. The results management component is concerned with comparing
performance with plan (both strategic and operational)
and ensuring the achievement of results. Thus, although
each component serves a different purpose, they are highly
integrated.

In Figure 1.2, the principal elements that make up
each component are outlined. The purpose of this diagram

Figure 1.2. Integrated Planning Process Elements.

is to provide the CEO and the planning team with an understanding of the total planning process. This diagram, with its outline, can serve as an excellent communications tool for developing a similar understanding of the planning process throughout the organization.

The strategic plan is the starting point for your organization's planning process. Strategic planning is, by its very nature, broad based and conceptual. It deals with the future in terms of strategy, long-term objectives, and integrated programs for accomplishing these objectives. The strategic plan also addresses the critical issues facing your organization in the future. For example, a medium-sized apparel manufacturer with a well-known brand name made a strategic decision several years ago to move aggressively into production of clothing under house labels (such as Sears, J. C. Penney, and Macy's) while continuing production under its own brand name. This required planning for such things as substantially increased production requirements, a dramatic change in marketing and sales approach, and significantly lower profit margins from the sale of house brands, among other critical issues.

Primary responsibility for developing the strategic plan rests with the CEO and the planning team (those involved in the strategic planning process). This effort is usually undertaken during the first and second quarters of the fiscal year, which allows ample time for completion or updating of the plan prior to developing the organization's operational plan. This is important because they are two completely different planning processes and are undertaken at different times of the year.

Many organizations attempt to do strategic and operational planning at the same time. This is rarely, if ever, successful. When both strategic and operational issues are discussed, the urgency of operational issues tends to dominate. Strategic planning requires considerable analysis and broad-gauged thinking on the part of the CEO and the planning team. Operational planning, on the other hand, is more specific and detailed and requires considerable time and effort by middle and first line management. For example, the operational plan for the apparel manufacturer referenced earlier included the creation, acquisition, and/or subcontracting of additional production facilities, the specialized training of marketing and sales personnel, and the development of a faster and more reliable distribution system. The focus of the operational plan is implementation and results. The focus of the strategic plan is concept and direction.

The operational plan, the middle component, plays a different role in the organization's planning process. Whereas the focus of strategic planning is on what business you should be in and the direction in which you should be going, the operational plan focuses very specifically on how the organization is going to get there. Typically, the time frame for the operational plan is one year, and it is developed during the third or fourth quarter. The primary purpose of this plan is to achieve the results outlined during the first year of the strategic plan. During the first year, for example, our apparel manufacturer concentrated on getting a few major accounts in chains where their brand name was not a stock item.

The third component, results management (or corporate performance and control), provides the CEO and the planning team an ongoing mechanism for monitoring implementation and results of both the strategic and operational plans. Whereas the first two components address the development of plans, results management is primarily concerned with plan execution, including the functions of reporting, controlling, and modifying the plans in order to meet the desired results. (This required our apparel manufacturer to establish more stringent financial controls in addition to reviewing and revising action plans on a frequent basis to ensure that required milestones were met.) Also, the activities that take place here are ongoing, as opposed to those of the strategic and operational plans, which are developed during specific periods of the year. To make planning a living, ongoing process within your organization, particular attention and emphasis must be given to results management. Incidentally, the apparel manufacturer used in the examples was able to make the transition to producing the house brands while maintaining its name-brand business. It ended up tripling its sales volume in five years, including an increase in its gross margin.

The CEO needs to be the chief architect of the Integrated Planning Process, which everyone in the organization understands and in which everyone participates. An important ingredient is the active involvement and commitment of the people within the organization. As the people who need to make the organization more successful become better informed about, and more actively involved in, the various planning steps, their commitment to achieving significant results will become substantial. Planning is a people process, and our focus is on making it work at all levels, starting with the senior executive team.

## How Does the Strategic Plan Fit into the Integrated Planning Process?

As we have indicated, the strategic plan cannot be developed in isolation from the operational plan and results management. Development of the strategic plan is done at a specific time, whereas implementation of this plan is only possible through the other two components of the Integrated Planning Process.

The primary role of the strategic plan is to provide the front-end focus and direction to the entire organization's planning efforts. Managers in an organization that has a strong operational plan going in the wrong direction will be frustrated in their efforts to achieve long-term, consistent results. They may achieve outstanding success for a while, but there will be a diminishing return over a longer time period. For example, how many of the highly successful CB (citizens band) radio producers of the early to mid 1970s are still around today? On the other hand, organizations that have a balanced planning process achieve consistent results over extended periods. One such example is

General Electric, which has a long tradition of both strategic and operational planning. Their results speak for themselves. There are also prime examples of companies in both the airline and telephone industries that have survived and prospered under deregulation as well as many that were unable to make the transition. Those with a balance of both strategic and operational planning generally have fared much better during this period.

## What Are the Elements of a Strategic Plan, and How Do They Fit Together?

A strategic plan is made up of seven elements: organization mission, strategic analysis, strategy, long-term objectives, integrated programs, financial projections, and the executive summary. Each is essential to the successful development and implementation of the plan. They can be likened to the parts of the human body. Although certain parts, such as the heart or lungs, may require more attention than others periodically, a lack of attention to any part could prove damaging or even fatal.

One approach to clarifying the elements of a strategic plan and how they fit together is illustrated in Figure 1.3. By addressing the questions *what, why, where, when,* and *how* as they apply to the first five elements of the strategic plan, the logic of the sequence becomes more evident.

Figure 1.3. Elements of the Strategic Plan.

| | | |
|---|---|---|
| Organization Mission | addresses | What |
| Strategic Analysis | addresses | Why |
| Strategy | addresses | Where |
| Long-term Objectives | addresses | When and How |
| Integrated Programs | addresses | When and How |
| Financial Projections and Executive Summary | incorporate | Portions of Each of the First Five Elements |

*1. Organization Mission.* The organization mission is the starting point of the strategic plan. It forms the foundation from which all the other strategic plan elements emanate. A mission statement identifies the basic concept of the organization. It provides a focal point for identifying an organization's purpose, the reason for its existence. A mission statement should develop a common vision with which all people associated with the organization can identify.

Each of the other six elements of the strategic plan needs to be in direct support of the mission statement. In terms of Figure 1.3, the primary function of the mission statement is to address the *what* questions. What business should the organization be in? What is the basic nature and concept of the organization? What is the philosophical basis for its existence?

*2. Strategic Analysis.* Strategic analysis is the data base of the strategic plan. It includes an analysis of the external and internal factors that are likely to have the greatest impact on the future of the organization. This leads to identification and prioritization of critical issues that need to be addressed in the plan and to conclusions for resolving these issues.

Strategic analysis is the most time-consuming element in the process. Because the strategic plan is by nature a conceptual plan, there needs to be a solid data base to support the key concerns. Strategic analysis addresses the *why* questions. Why does this mission make sense? Why is this the correct strategy? Why are these the appropriate long-term objectives and integrated programs?

*3. Strategy.* The element of strategy specifies the direction of the organization. This description may be different from your perception of the word *strategy*. As used here, *strategy* addresses the *where* dimension of strategic planning rather than the *how*. Strategy is designed to position the organization for the future rather than focus on how it will get there. This is a crucial distinction, which is developed further in Chapter Five. A strategy statement should either confirm the current direction or establish a new direction based on the organization's mission and strategic analysis. Proper strategy development is a very challenging aspect of strategic planning.

*4. Long-Term Objectives.* Long-term objectives identify the strategic results required to carry out the organization's mission and strategy. These strategic results are broad based and reflect what the organization wishes to have or become in such areas as profitability, growth, diversification, new products, and new markets.

*5. Integrated Programs.* Integrated programs represent the major cross-functional actions required to carry out the strategy and accomplish the long-term objectives. The term *integrated programs* was carefully chosen. This is the point in the strategic planning process where integration among the various functional units needs to occur. For example, a new product development program requires close integration among engineering, production, marketing, and sales, at the very least.

The purpose of integrated programs is to ensure the translation of broad-based, long-term objectives into specific results. It is the point in the strategic planning process at which individual accountability is assigned to make sure results will be accomplished. In order for the strategic plan to be fully implemented, the integrated programs must be developed in sufficient detail for the CEO to monitor and track progress.

Integrated programs also provide an important link between the strategic and operational plans. These programs develop the broad framework within which short-term objectives, detailed action plans, and controls can be formulated to achieve operational results.

Both the long-term objectives and integrated programs address the questions of *how* and *when.* How and when will the mission and strategy be carried out? How

and when will results be achieved? How and when will resources be allocated? How and when will progress be reviewed?

   *6. Financial Projections.* Financial projections summarize the planned financial results and the measures of
performance required to implement the plan. The purpose
of this strategic plan element is to provide an organized
format for presenting all the financial information in one
place. The financial implications of the strategic plan need
to be understood by both those who approve and those
who implement the plan. As the plan is developed, the financial numbers must be realistic and make sense. Unlike
the other elements of the strategic plan, financial projections are a compilation of information obtained from strategic analysis, long-term objectives, and integrated programs.

   *7. Executive Summary.* The executive summary
personalizes the plan from the CEO's viewpoint. It presents
the issues, tests the logic, and pulls the plan sharply into
focus. It enables the CEO to communicate the executive
vision of the organization's future.

   The strategic plan framework is shown in Figure 1.4.
The plan starts with a broad and open-ended approach to
developing an organization mission statement. Once the
mission statement has been documented, the focus begins
to narrow. The next step is to complete a strategic analysis
of those issues and areas likely to have the greatest impact
on fulfilling the organization's mission. Following strategic
analysis, the focus is narrowed further to selecting or confirming the particular strategy required to fulfill the mission. These first three steps place heavy emphasis on the
strategic thinking that must take place if the total planning effort is to be successful.
   Next is the selection or confirmation of those long-
term objectives required to fulfill the mission and carry
out the strategy. As indicated in the diagram, selection of

Figure 1.4. Strategic Plan Framework.

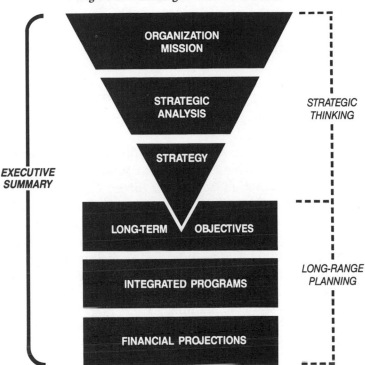

these long-term objectives is both the culmination of strategic thinking and the start of long-range planning. The primary purpose of strategic thinking is to make sure that the *right* long-term objectives have been selected—those that will lead the organization toward the fulfillment of its mission and the pursuit of the particular strategy selected.

Once long-term objectives have been selected, specific broad-based integrated programs required to achieve these objectives must be identified. The next step is to complete the financial projections, which are the financial results required to support the strategic plan. In a sense, they form the base of the strategic plan framework. These three steps represent what has been known, historically, as long-range planning. However, without the strategic thinking that occurs during the first three steps, long-range planning is inadequate at best and could be disastrous if it were to lead in the wrong direction.

The final step in the process is preparation of the CEO's executive summary, which encompasses the entire strategic plan.

## What Is the Most Effective Approach to Developing a Strategic Plan?

Our experience suggests that the approach to strategic planning that achieves the most consistent results within a reasonable period of time involves a series of open, wide-ranging, and results-oriented executive team planning meetings. Each of these meetings needs to be structured to address one or more of the strategic planning elements shown in Figure 1.4. The number of meetings may vary from as few as four to as many as eight, depending on the complexity of the plan and the experience level of the team in doing strategic planning. These meetings generally represent a time commitment of six to ten days over a three- to six-month period. Effective strategic planning is a time-consuming process. It should not be entered into lightly.

One reason this approach works is because of the equal emphasis placed on both the process of planning and the content of the strategic plan. The process of planning is defined as the means by which the plan is developed. It includes the selection of the planning team, clarification of team member roles, careful structuring of the planning meetings, and the guiding of the team through the process itself. The thinking, dialoguing, confronting, revising, and consensus-seeking that goes on during this process is frequently as valuable as the plan itself in shaping the future of the organization. The content of the strategic plan is defined by the seven elements described above.

Both the content and process of the strategic plan are of equal importance. Your strategic plan needs to have a sound, logical structure within which the various plan elements can be developed and documented. The strategic framework provided in Figure 1.4 provides such a readily understandable structure.

## In Summary

The strategic plan is the first of three major components of the Integrated Planning Process and is the primary focus of this book. The other two components, the operational plan and results management, will be covered in subsequent volumes. The strategic plan establishes the basic nature and direction of the organization and contains seven elements: organization mission, strategic analysis, strategy, long-term objectives, integrated programs, financial projections, and the executive summary. Each of these elements serves a different, though related, purpose and is addressed individually in this book.

Development of the strategic plan requires the active involvement and commitment of the CEO (chief executive officer or whoever is the key decision maker) and the executive team. Eventually, other managers throughout the organization must become involved and committed as they develop their own plans for supporting the total organization's efforts. How to get commitment to strategic planning is dealt with in Chapter Two.

# 2

 Gaining Organizational
Commitment to
Strategic Planning

Is strategic planning an activity that key managers in your organization look forward to? Does it rank as one of the most exhilarating events of the year—a truly scintillating experience? Although these questions may be a bit unrealistic, the development of your organization's strategic plan can and should be an experience that is both exciting and productive for participating managers and should have a tremendous payoff for them personally as well as for the organization. Why is it that managers in some organizations see participation in the strategic planning process as one of their most meaningful management experiences while managers in other organizations avoid it completely or enter into the process reluctantly, putting forth a minimum amount of effort? Why is management commitment to strategic planning necessary, and how do you get it?

## Why Is Commitment Necessary?

The success of your strategic planning effort will be in direct proportion to the degree of commitment your key managers make to the plan and the planning process. As pointed out in Chapter One, effective strategic planning requires a significant investment of time and energy. It is people who make the plan a reality. The plan must be seen as a living document which will be implemented by your key managers. Consequently, they must believe in both the plan and the way it was developed if they are to give it their best effort. With a well-developed plan and the total commitment of those managers who must make it work, miracles can, and frequently do, happen.

## Where Does Commitment Start?

Commitment to a course of action can come only from within the individual. It cannot be imposed from without. External pressure may lead to compliance, but true commitment is a choice on the part of an individual to do something. It requires a personal conviction that the action being considered is worthwhile and will be beneficial to those affected. In other words, if you want managers in your organization to be committed to strategic planning, they must see it as being beneficial to them personally as well as to the organization.

## What Keeps Individual Managers from Being Committed to Strategic Planning?

Here are some typical reactions from people who do not appear to be committed to strategic planning. Let's examine some of the feelings behind these reactions to determine what can be done to make sure effective strategic planning becomes a reality in their lives.

*"We don't have time to plan!"* This usually represents a feeling of frustration in individuals who perceive planning, particularly strategic planning, as one more task being heaped on an already overloaded schedule. Some of the reasons they feel the pressure of time are that other important responsibilities may have to be put aside, they don't feel appreciated for their efforts, they are unclear about what is expected, or they feel there is no useful purpose to be served by the effort.

Let's not kid ourselves; managers must devote considerable amounts of time to the planning process. But experience shows that managers who do practice effective planning end up with substantially better use of their time as a result. Furthermore, the benefit to the organization in results achieved from effective planning makes the time invested one of the greatest bargains around.

*"How can we plan when things are changing so fast?"* This typically reflects both a reaction to rapidly changing circumstances and a concern that plans, once established, will be cast in concrete and there will be no allowance for modifications based on changing circumstances. This is especially true of strategic planning and its long-term objectives. A prime example would be in the electronics industry, where rapid changes in technology resulted in the virtual obsolescence of certain companies' products. Some of these companies have been able to adapt quickly, others have gone into a survival mode, and some have not survived.

It must be clearly understood at the outset that a set of plans is established on the best available information at the time. However, it is virtually a certainty that unexpected events, new opportunities, changing resource requirements, technological breakthroughs, or changes in the marketplace, to name a few circumstances, will happen during the period of any established plan, strategic or operational. The value in having a plan is that, when changes are indicated, they can be made with full awareness that this change is taking place rather than being a result of just drifting in the wind. When managers can accept the fact that their plans can be modified to reflect legitimate changing circumstances, they are much more likely to put the effort forth to ensure that meaningful plans are established.

*"We don't get paid for planning; we get paid for results!"* Most managers tend to be action oriented. This frequently leads to a sense of frustration when time and effort are expended in areas that are not perceived to be

directly related to one's primary job. This is frequently re-inforced by members of higher-level management who give recognition only for specific results or who express excessive concern over short-term problem issues. The focus needs to be not on results alone, but on the right results. Effective planning is needed to ensure that we are concerned with future, as well as present, success.

*"Who needs strategic planning? We're doing O.K. now."* For a period of time, many organizations, particularly when still rather small, achieve phenomenal success based on strong entrepreneurial effort, a new and unique product or service, and/or extremely favorable market conditions. It is natural for them to assume that such success will continue. However, it only takes one major setback for managers to recognize the fragility of such a position. For example, skyrocketing interest rates turned a bonanza into bankruptcy for many real estate investors in the late 1970s. Likewise, several fast-growing oil-related companies suffered incredible reverses as a result of plummeting oil prices in the mid 1980s.

Visible strong commitment to strategic planning from the top level of the organization is essential if other managers within the organization are to feel this commitment. History has proven time and again that success without a clear sense of direction tends to be short-lived. Once managers can see that the future of the organization—and their subsequent reward and position within it—are dependent on initiating long-range plans even while at the height of success, they are much more likely to feel an appropriate sense of commitment to the strategic planning effort.

### What Can Top Management Do to Encourage Total Organization Commitment to Strategic Planning?

Clearly, the CEO and other executives must provide the leadership if there is to be real commitment to strategic planning throughout the organization. Executive leadership includes the following:

1. *Visible commitment from above.* This senior-level commitment must demonstrate a willingness to invest the time necessary to do an effective job of planning and to regularly review results against those plans. The various roles related to strategic planning are described later in this chapter. Senior executives must ask questions related to both long-term organizational direction and short-term results, such as current sales and delivery problems.

2. *Clear and realistic expectations,* including provision for changing circumstances. It is crucial for senior management to establish challenging expectations that will move the organization in the direction they have determined is appropriate. Long-term objectives and integrated programs that derive from these expectations need to be challenging but must have a reasonably good probability of successful completion. If managers feel that they can influence the nature of the results expected and that they have it within their ability and power to realize that achievement, they are far more likely to put forth the effort that comes from true commitment.

3. *Coaching/training in planning process methodology.* There is a distinct body of knowledge that is related to strategic planning and there are specific skills that can be acquired. First, all those involved must have a clear understanding of the terminology used and the precise methodology to be followed. Although this terminology should be as simple and straightforward as possible, managers must understand what they will be expected to do in their strategic planning efforts, which frequently requires some training. The skills of planning are best learned through actual application during the planning meetings themselves. These skills can also be reinforced through ongoing coaching during the planning and review cycle. Without formal attention to the knowledge and skills required, it is virtually inevitable that many managers will resist put-

ting forth the amount of effort required to represent a true commitment.

4. *Top priority attention* to strategic planning efforts during high concentration periods. Strategic planning requires concentrated thought. If managers are expected to put significant effort into determining where the organization is going, then some provision must be made for shifting other responsibilities during that period. If those involved are expected to carry on all of their normal duties, cope with unexpected occurrences, and do a thorough job in their strategic planning efforts, a certain amount of frustration may develop. During the strategic planning period, there is frequently an opportunity to delegate appropriate responsibility and authority to others within the organization, a step that can provide a growth experience for them while it relieves the planning team member of certain duties.

5. *Minimization of paperwork*. Although there will inevitably be a certain amount of paperwork necessary to develop and sustain the strategic planning process, it can and should be controlled. You do not need several volumes of typewritten material to have an effective strategic plan. Nothing will put a damper on commitment faster than an avalanche of paperwork that accountable managers consider an added burden.

6. *Clarification of roles* of the planning team. Strategic planning is a team process, and each team member plays a specific role. When these roles are clearly defined and team members understand what is expected of others as well as themselves, commitment is likely to follow.

## What Are the Key Roles of the Planning Team?

Let's examine each of the key roles of the planning team and some of the specific activities in which they need to be involved.

1. *The chief executive officer* (or key decision maker) should be perceived as the person providing direct and active leadership to the strategic plan. The CEO's primary

strategic planning duties include approval of and, in most cases, direct involvement in such things as:

- development of the organization mission
- identification and prioritization of critical issues
- development of strategy
- identification and articulation of organization long-term objectives
- creation of the executive summary

Naturally, there will be other areas where the CEO needs to be deeply involved as well. Even though much of the detail work may be carried out by others, the CEO has to provide the visibility and leadership in making sure the strategic plan is developed and implemented.

The CEO is the principal planner for the organization and the person ultimately accountable to the board of directors, the parent company, or other higher-level groups for determining where the organization should be going and ensuring that it gets there.

2. *The chief operating officer (COO),* when it is someone other than the CEO, frequently has responsibility for the creation, implementation, and achievement of the organization's operational plan and is accountable to the CEO for its validity and accuracy. In addition, the COO is normally an adviser to the CEO and a member of the planning team assisting the CEO in carrying out the duties described for that office.

3. *The senior executive team* is generally made up of five to seven key executives including the CEO, COO, and major department heads plus one or two key staff advisers. Members of the team function as an extension of the CEO and, as such, primarily represent the total organization and, secondarily, their particular organizational units. They participate in many, if not all, of the planning activities identified for the CEO. However, it is important that ground rules be established to ensure that the members of the executive team, at that point, are wearing their

"total organization" hats, not those of the specific functions they represent.

4. *The board of directors,* in most organizations, delegates to the CEO the responsibility for the creation, implementation, and achievement of the organization's strategic and operational plans but retains the right of review and final approval. Board members, individually or as a group, may offer advice and counsel on key strategic issues, but their involvement in the strategic plan normally is limited to the establishment of broad guidelines in terms of organizational direction and financial projections.

5. *The planning coordinator* is someone designated within the organization to make sure that the strategic plan comes together. Frequently, it is a member of the executive team and, particularly in smaller organizations, the role may be assumed by the CEO. It needs to be filled by someone with good administrative skills who wants the job. Normally, unless it is the CEO, the coordinator does not have approval authority but may perform any or all of the following duties:

- establishing and monitoring the planning schedule
- coordinating and handling logistics of planning meetings
- documenting and distributing meeting records

6. *The coach/facilitator* ensures an organized and participative planning process. In order for the planning process to be productive, this person should be someone who does not have a major vested interest in the outcome. Although a member of the senior executive team may have the knowledge and skill to perform that role, that team member needs to be free to take an advocacy position on certain issues and to express convictions during discussions. To be effective, a coach/facilitator must remain neutral while guiding the discussion.

The coach/facilitator role is frequently filled by a consultant, either internal or external (or a combination of the two), who has strong knowledge of strategic planning and good facilitation skills. This person must have both the respect of participating executives and personal confidence because it may be necessary at times to confront individual members of the team. An internal consultant often brings an in-depth knowledge of the organization and generally is more accessible than an external consultant. An external consultant brings a broader and more diverse experience and often has greater impact on required actions because of the timing of visits (which frequently serve as deadlines for certain team members). An effective internal/external consulting team brings the best of both worlds. The coach/facilitator may perform any or all of the following duties:

- planning system design
- CEO coaching/counseling
- planning meeting design
- executive/managerial training
- planning meeting facilitation
- meeting summarization
- plan documentation

7. *An internal planning staff,* if there is one, is not responsible for the strategic plan. That is, and must be, an executive management responsibility. The internal planning staff gathers information and performs preliminary analyses in such areas as market and industry trends. They may also perform some of the duties described as appropriate to the roles of planning coordinator and coach/facilitator. Although the trend in prior years has been to build large corporate planning staffs who developed most of the planning documents, recently these staffs have been drastically reduced in size. Planning specialists are now advising and counseling line managers and providing specific analysis.

Naturally, all managers within an organization, as well as many individual employees, need to be involved in, or informed about, the strategic plan. In some cases, strategic planning responsibilities may be quite extensive, in effect a miniversion of what takes place at the senior levels; in others, it may just require familiarization in order to meet organizational objectives. Persons at all levels within an organization need to accept their responsibility for planning as it applies to their specific areas. However, this book is primarily directed at the responsibilities of the key people described in this chapter.

## In Summary

A key ingredient in the planning process is commitment of people. This requires (1) visible commitment from above, (2) clear and realistic expectations, including a provision for changing circumstances, (3) coaching/training in planning process methodology, (4) top priority attention to strategic planning efforts, (5) minimization of paperwork, and (6) clarification of roles of the planning team. This begins with a clear definition of the CEO's role followed by definition of roles of other team members. With a precise understanding and acceptance of the importance of the strategic planning process, the first step is taken toward achieving total organization commitment.

# 3

 Defining
the Organization's
Mission

Developing your organization's mission statement is the first step in the strategic planning process. This statement forms the foundation for the rest of the plan and provides a common vision for the total organization. Consequently, it should not be seen primarily as a public relations document developed by a staff group to create an image for the outside world. Nor should it be written by a single person, even the CEO, for rubber-stamp approval. It requires the active involvement of planning team members to ensure that all pertinent factors are examined and that there is team ownership of the final document. For the planning process to be truly *integrated,* the mission statement needs to provide a clear focus so that all other planning steps can be tested against it for relevance. It needs to be entered into with clear thought and ample discussion to ensure that it becomes a true statement of the basic concept of the organization.

## What Is a Mission Statement?

Very simply, an organization's mission statement describes the nature and concept of the organization's future business. It establishes what the organization plans to do, and for whom, plus the major philosophical premises under which it will operate. Primary among the reasons for an organization having such a statement are:

1.  to ensure consistency and clarity of purpose throughout the organization
2.  to provide a point of reference for all major planning decisions
3.  to gain commitment from those within the organization through clear communication of the nature and concept of the organization's business
4.  to gain understanding and support from those people outside the organization who are important to its success

Although in this chapter we concentrate primarily on how to develop a mission statement, we need to keep in mind the various uses to which the mission can be put once it has been satisfactorily developed. Its principal application is as an internal guide for all major decision makers within the organization so plans that are developed can be tested for compatibility with the total organization's mission. Without a clear statement of purpose for the entire organization, it is easy for resources to become diffused and for individual units to operate completely independently, often at cross purposes. In other words, the mission statement should be a visible document that can enable virtually everybody within the organization to focus their efforts in a manner that is supportive. One CEO we know makes it a practice about once a month to stand in the parking lot as employees are coming to work and ask several at random if they understand the company's mission and objectives. Fortunately, this particular CEO does not have an intimidating manner, so this method gives him good feedback in terms of how well understood the corporate plans are. Furthermore, because it is common knowledge that he does this, most employees find it to their advantage to be thoroughly familiar with the company's mission and objectives.

Externally, the organization's mission statement provides clear communication to such groups as customers, suppliers, and the financial community, as well as the board of directors and stockholders. Although its primary purpose is not that of a public relations document, it can serve effectively in that manner if it has been properly prepared.

### How Is a Mission Statement Developed?

An effective way of starting development of a mission statement, or of reviewing an existing one, is to schedule an off-site planning meeting for that purpose. The first step is to circulate to each individual on the planning team copies of the worksheet "Clarifying an Organization's Mission," that appears at the end of this chapter. Team members should be requested to complete the worksheet on their own in advance of the planning meeting, without discussing it with other members of the team. This is to encourage as much independent thinking as possible and avoid the bandwagon or me-too type of response. The worksheet is designed to get team members to look at the big picture of the total organization rather than merely their own areas of responsibility. Although answers to all the questions will not necessarily be included in the mission statement, discussion of them is a significant early step in strategic thinking. We believe it is important for people to write down their answers to these questions as a form of crystallizing their own thinking.

At the planning meeting, the team members address one question at a time. Team members read off their answers to each question. These responses are posted on a chart pad for all to see. The only discussion permitted during this posting is related to clarification of meaning, not to the validity of the statement. (An alternative to this approach is to have the worksheets turned in to the coach/ facilitator, who posts the various answers on chart pad paper in advance of the meeting.) Once all answers to a given question have been posted, the meeting is opened for discussion. The coach/facilitator draws out the various points of view, encouraging the expression of differences and the generation of additional ideas that may be triggered through the process. The role of the coach/facilitator is especially critical here because it is up to that individual to make sure that innovative thinking takes place, that no individual dominates the discussion, and hopefully, that the group reaches an agreement on the key factors to be included in the mission statement. A minimum of a half day should be devoted to this effort, with the potential of a full day if there is a wide diversity of opinions on the part of team members. Allow whatever time is necessary to reach consensus. Shortchanging this step will seriously impair the rest of the planning process.

Let's examine the questions on the worksheet individually and explore some of the implications of each.

*1. What business should we be in?* The answer to this question is not nearly as obvious as many people would think. One of the problems that frequently occurs in organizations is that people tend to fall into the "this is the way we've always done it" mode. The organization has to start with where its current thinking is. However, this may or may not be where they want to be in the future. There have been some classic cases of companies, and even industries, that maintained such a narrow view of the nature of their business that they ultimately allowed themselves to become obsolete. Others have made a successful transition when their primary business became endangered. For example, a major shift saw passenger ship companies move from a posture of being in the oceangoing transportation business to becoming the ultimate in luxury entertainment when the airlines took over international travel. Several large tobacco companies diversified into other fields when it became evident that antismoking pressure was not going to go away.

One way to start is by taking a look at the industry in which the organization is, or should be, represented and then looking at the organization's particular niche within that industry. You could also specify what the organization has been charged to accomplish, both financially and in terms of its service to the marketplace, by its board of directors, parent company, or other higher-level body.

*2. Why do we exist (what is our basic purpose)?* Although, in many organizations, profit or financial return is perceived as the reason for existence, it is rarely, if ever, the sole reason. There are other purposes in addition to the financial ones to which many organizations aspire. These may be related to such things as service to a customer base, contribution to technology, recognition for achievement, and provision of a creative outlet for founders and/or employees.

*3. What is unique or distinctive about our organization?* Every organization, if it is to continue to be successful, needs to have one or more characteristics about it that sets it apart from other organizations engaged in a similar business. This needs to be determined for marketing purposes as well as for giving direction and focus to the organization's efforts. Sometimes what appears to be a disadvantage may be turned into a distinct plus in this area by proper identification and positioning. Some familiar illustrations of this point are the campaign by Avis as "number two" in the car rental business, 7-Up being positioned as the "un-Cola," and Chrysler's comeback after financial near disaster.

Here are a few of the various factors that could be determined to be unique (one of a kind) or distinctive (clearly set apart from others) in some way:

| | |
|---|---|
| proprietary products/services | key individuals/groups |
| concentration (or diversity) of products/services | method of sale |
| | method of distribution |
| geographic concentration (or dispersion) | types of support services |
| | warranties |
| types of markets/customers | legislative mandate |
| unique capabilities/processes | franchise operation |

*4. Who are our principal customers, clients, or users?*
Many organizations have a series of customers whose needs
have to be satisfied before their products or services reach
the ultimate user. A manufacturer of consumer goods, for
example, usually has to depend on a retail outlet (its direct
customer) to get products directly to the eventual pur-
chasers (their ultimate users). A hospital normally can
serve a patient (its ultimate user) only if a doctor (its direct customer) places the patient in that hospital. Although
there are some exceptions, most manufacturers of computer peripherals recognize that their principal customers
are original equipment manufacturers (OEMs), through
whose efforts their products eventually reach the end
users. Both types of customers need to be identified, when
applicable, in order to properly define business focus.

We have inserted alternative words, *customers, clients,* and *users,* so you can select whatever term is appropriate to your business. However, we feel it is very important to keep the concept of customer in front of us,
regardless of the business in which we are engaged. A customer is someone whose needs and wants we are in business to satisfy. We address customers, rather than markets,
here in order to clearly identify the tangible recipients of
our services. Getting a clear articulation of who these customers are and the order in which their needs and wants
must be satisfied is a critical step in determining how the
business should be projected.

*5. What are our principal products/services, present
and future?* This identifies the primary deliverables that our
customers, clients, or users expect to receive from us. Typically, we think in terms of groups of products or services
rather than individual items. Supporting services, such as
customer training or maintenance, should be identified if
they are revenue producing or if they represent a substantial amount of resource allocation. Products or services
that may be offered to specific customers on an as-needed
basis, but are not a part of the mainstream, normally
would not be included here. If there are additional major

products or services that should become a part of the organization's future, they should be identified here as well.

*6. What are our principal market segments, present and future?* Market segments are identified in broad categories, not in the detail that might be done in a market analysis. They represent groups of customers or potential customers that can be segregated on the basis of such things as geography, type and size of industry, occupation, age, and economic status.

*7. What are our principal outlets/distribution channels, present and future?* Outlets and distribution channels represent how we reach the end user and could include such things as direct sales, marketing representatives, distributors, direct mail, centralized or decentralized storage, and retail outlets (our own or others).

*8. What is different about our business from what it was between three and five years ago?* What substantial factors have had a significant impact in *changing* the nature of our business from what it was earlier? These would include changes that have taken place in our industry, marketplace, or environment that we may not have satisfactorily addressed as yet. Such things as technology, markets, competition, organizational structure, financing, labor mix, and product/service mix may be identified here.

*9. What is likely to be different about our business three to five years in the future?* Identify those things that are inevitable, such as demographic changes, and those things that we can make happen and should give serious attention to, such as our position in the marketplace. Many of the factors considered in question 8 need to be addressed here as well. Team members are encouraged to do some blue-sky thinking at this point, generating a number of ideas that may or may not be valid. In addition to what people identify in their premeeting preparation, the use of brainstorming at this stage frequently generates innovative ideas that are worth considering.

*10. What are our principal economic concerns, and how are they measured?* Every organization, to survive and be successful, has certain specific economic concerns that must be satisfied. If we are in a profit-making organization, we need to clarify what that means. The mission statement should include a commitment to profitability and/or growth. There must be a clear and common understanding among team members as to just exactly how the concept of profit will be approached. Profit is the financial result of an organization's effort and may be measured by such indicators as return on assets/equity/invested capital, percent of sales, and gross margin. Growth represents the size in terms of sales, capacity, diversity, and the like and can be measured in absolute amounts or as a rate of growth. For those organizations in the public sector, or those who consider themselves as not-for-profit, a concept such as cost-effective use of available resources or increased service at no increase in cost is an important consideration.

*11. What philosophical issues are important to our organization's future?* These are clear statements of major belief that directly affect the way your organization will do business. Those that are especially strong influencers should be included as a part of the mission statement and could include reference to such areas as:

organizational image
leadership in industry/profession/community
environmental impact
innovation/risk-taking
quality
productivity
management approach

The purpose of this question is to highlight major factors affecting future management decisions. For example, a company concerned about the environment might state that "we will not knowingly introduce any product or process that has a destructive impact on the world in which we live."

*12. What special considerations do we have in regard to the following stakeholders (as applicable)?*

owners/stockholders/investors/constituents
board of directors
parent organization
legislative bodies
employees
customers/clients/users
suppliers
general public
others (specify)

The term *stakeholders* refers to any group of people that has a vested interest in the organization's future and that may need special consideration. If there are particular items that need to be addressed either in the mission statement or at some point in the strategic planning process, they need to be identified in order to become a part of the related discussions.

## How Is the Mission Statement Prepared?

When the discussion of the worksheet takes place at the planning meeting, the coach/facilitator leads the team through a consensus exercise designed to bring about agreement on each key factor. In reviewing each of the factors, a decision is reached as to which items need to be included in the mission statement and which items belong elsewhere in the planning process. One approach is for the coach/facilitator, with the assistance of one or two team members, to draft a preliminary mission statement incorporating those factors the group has designated for inclusion. It is then reviewed and refined by the team.

A mission statement is one-half to one page in length. It normally includes an umbrella statement (fifteen to thirty words) that identifies the conceptual nature of the business in which the organization expects to be engaged in the future.

Following that, there may be a statement that opens with something like "In support of this mission, this organization is committed to" followed by a limited series of itemized statements of specific philosophy and overall operation similar to those shown in the examples in the next section of this chapter. This becomes the basis for how the organization will be functioning and how departments or units within the organization can determine their own roles, missions, and objectives. It serves as a clear statement of the organization's perspective and how it wants to be perceived by all of its various stakeholders. A word of caution—don't include anything in your statement of mission that you are not willing to back up with action. If any item in a mission statement is perceived as not really reflecting the way you do business, it will destroy the credibility of your planning efforts. This is why dialogue among the planning team is especially critical before publication of the mission statement.

## What Are Some Examples of Mission Statements?

Here are some mission statements adapted from those of actual organizations in both the private and public sectors. The specific terminology selected in each is especially appropriate to these organizations and would not necessarily be applicable to other similar organizations.

XXXX is in business to supply technically innovative hardware and software I/O solutions to the OEM computer market that provide a long-term benefit to our customers and a long-term return to our investors.

In support of this, we are committed to

- being recognized by our customers for being responsive and oriented to their needs
- being recognized for being a technically superior and innovative supplier of high-quality products
- being recognized by our employees and the business community for excellence and integrity in managing the company's business
- providing an environment for achieving personal excellence and growth for all our employees

The primary mission of the XXXX Group is to assist our clients in achieving cost-effective results from their employee benefit planning through the marketing, implementation, and administration of creative, individually-designed plans.

The mission of XXXX County is to economically and efficiently provide and manage delivery systems for diverse programs and services to meet basic human needs.

In support of this, we are committed to

- serving as an agent for the federal and state governments to fulfill mandated programs
- providing optional community services as determined by the county board
- providing programs and services in the most cost-effective manner
- encouraging citizen awareness, participa-

tion, and involvement in county government

- utilizing community resources as a vehicle for good government

XXXX supplies products that provide environmentally safe solutions to customer problems associated with the reliable transfer or control of fluids.

The mission of the Planning Process Group is to provide transferable planning process technology (Integrated Planning Process) that focuses on organizational results for the CEO and key decision makers.

In support of this, we are committed to

- a network with an established CEO/decision maker base
- proprietary materials customized to network requirements
- a visible reputation for consistently achieving planning results
- accelerated financial and professional growth

## In Summary

The development of a statement of mission for the organization is the first, and one of the most critical, elements in the strategic plan. It forms a foundation from which all other management decisions must be made. It requires careful thought and preparation on the part of the planning team, with ample time allowed for the refinement of the various points of view that are likely to be expressed. Once such a statement has been clearly established and approved, it should remain constant for an extended

Figure 3.1. Clarifying an Organization's Mission.

1.  What business should we be in?

2.  Why do we exist (what is our basic purpose)?

3.  What is unique or distinctive about our organization?

4.  Who are our principal customers, clients, or users?

5.  What are our principal products/services, present and future?

6.  What are our principal market segments, present and future?

7.  What are our principal outlets/distribution channels, present and future?

8.  What is different about our business from what it was between three and five years ago?

9.  What is likely to be different about our business three to five years in the future?

10. What are our principal economic concerns, and how are they measured?

Figure 3.1. Clarifying an Organization's Mission, Cont'd.

11.   What philosophical issues are important to our organization's future?


12.   What special considerations do we have in regard to the following stakeholders (as applicable)?

- Owner/stockholders/investors/constituents


- Board of directors


- Parent organization


- Legislative bodies


- Employees


- Customers, clients, or users


- Suppliers


- General public


- Others (specify)

period of time unless there is a major change in the nature of the business or of the overall philosophy of the organization. The statement of organizational mission needs to be reviewed formally at least once a year as a part of the strategic planning process. It is a prerequisite to completing the next element, strategic analysis.

# 4

# Producing a
# Strategic Analysis

## What Is Strategic Analysis?

Strategic analysis forms the data base of the strategic plan. It is an in-depth examination of the external and internal environmental factors that are likely to have the greatest impact on the future of the organization. External factors include market segments, technology, competition, industry structure, and strategic opportunities and threats. Internal factors include financial resources, products and/or services, internal capabilities (such as manufacturing, engineering, research and development), and strategic strengths and limitations.

During the analysis process the following questions should be kept in mind:

1. Is the analysis bringing to the surface the truly critical issues facing the organization?
2. Are sufficient information and judgment being used to support the selection of and agreement on these issues?
3. Are these issues being thoroughly analyzed and discussed in terms of their root causes?
4. Is the analysis producing conclusions about these causes?

5.  Are these major conclusions clearly defensible both in-
    side and outside the organization?

Strategic analysis is the most time-consuming element in strategic planning. However, the time and effort
spent in this area will pay rich dividends in team understanding as well as in the quality of the strategic plan. In
fact, the strategic analysis section will be constantly reviewed and updated as an important data base for clarifying strategic issues on an ongoing basis.

## How Is Strategic Analysis Approached?

There are many approaches for undertaking a strategic analysis. The key is to follow a process that ensures
that a comprehensive analysis is undertaken with the active involvement of the CEO and the team. This analysis is
carried out in a systematic manner that allows for both in-
depth analysis and sufficient dialogue among team members.

A practical method for approaching strategic analysis is the use of critical issues. In this approach, critical
issues are defined early in the process, thereby avoiding
the possibility of the team being inundated by extraneous
information and analysis. It also helps the team focus attention on those areas that require in-depth analysis.

Initially, the purpose is to bring to the surface critical issues that presently reside within the minds of team
members. This initial free-flowing approach creates a cli-
mate that is not intimidating and that relies as much on
intuition and judgment as it does on facts and figures.
Everyone on the team is able to contribute to the analysis
process. This prevents the analysis from turning into a
form-completion exercise, a trap many organizations fall
into.

A critical issue is usually a complex situation, event,
or trend that is likely to make the difference between
achieving average or superior performance in the long run.
Although there are many important factors or trends that

might influence the organization's overall performance, there are usually only a few truly critical issues that will make a difference to its long-term success. Typical critical issues might include such things as product lines that have substantial long-term profit potential, major changes likely to take place in the marketplace, or significant competitors' strengths or weaknesses that might be exploited. For example, anticipation of the difficulties IBM would have with the introduction of the PC Jr. (personal computer) in 1984 enabled COMPAQ Computer to gain a substantial competitive advantage.

Factors that might identify critical issues include:

1.  Size of gap between past/present performance and future required performance. For example: "The record in new product sales shows an average of less than 5 percent of total sales in new products over the last three years. However, future requirements indicate a need to attain a level of 15 to 20 percent in sales from new products." This needed improvement may be of such a magnitude that it represents a critical issue for the organization.
2.  Impact on profitability and/or growth. Another guideline for determining a critical issue is to focus on those areas that have an impact of 25 percent or more on future profit/growth. For example: A potential technological development may render an entire product line obsolete, resulting in a substantial sales decline.
3.  Special requirements for accomplishing the organization's mission. These provide another source of critical issues. For example: What are the most important accomplishments needed to fulfill the mission? What barriers stand in the way of these accomplishments?

## How Is the Strategic Analysis Produced?

A sequence of five steps (diagrammed in Figure 4.1) must be taken by the CEO and the planning team to produce a strategic analysis.

**Figure 4.1. Sequence of Steps in Strategic Analysis.**

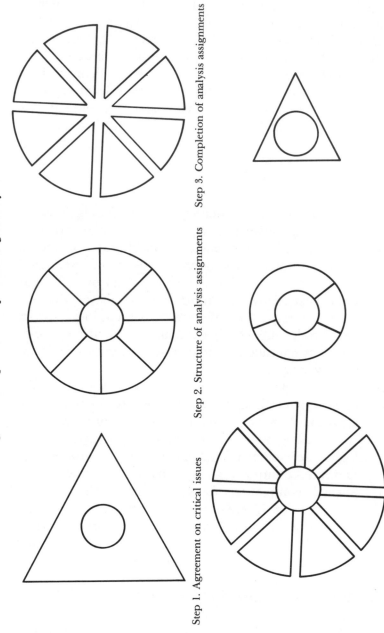

Step 1. Agreement on critical issues

Step 2. Structure of analysis assignments

Step 3. Completion of analysis assignments

Step 4. Presentation of analysis assignments

Step 5. Agreement on analysis and conclusions

Completed stategic analysis

*Step 1. Agreement on Critical Issues.* A number of critical issues may be apparent to the CEO and the team. If so, they must first be identified and then verified or removed as the analysis proceeds.

*Step 2. Structure of Analysis Assignments.* Assignments are structured through use of a situation analysis wheel, which is depicted in Figure 4.2. The shaded areas of the wheel represent external analysis; the light areas, internal analysis. External analysis refers to consideration of

Figure 4.2. Situation Analysis Wheel.

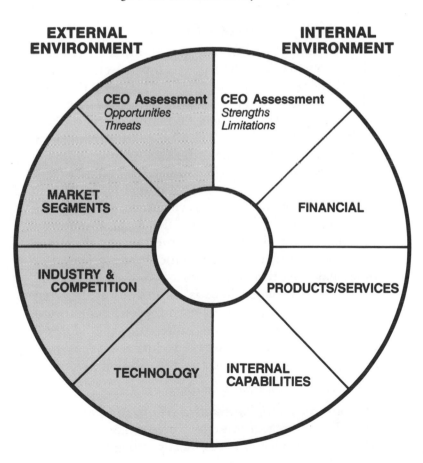

areas outside the organization that are likely to have a major impact on its future direction. Internal analysis refers to consideration of those factors inside the organization that can be expected to have a significant bearing on its direction.

The situation analysis wheel is aptly named. The reason for calling it a wheel is that it provides the planning team with a balance of quantitative and qualitative analysis assignments covering both their internal and external environments. Of the eight segments that comprise the situation analysis wheel, four represent the external environment and four the internal environment:

### External Environment

- *CEO assessment of external opportunities and threats.* This represents the CEO's personal perspective on outside challenges facing the organization; here those the CEO particularly wishes to pursue are highlighted.
- *Market segments.* This calls for an analysis of both present and future trends in relation to such things as demographics, geographical dispersion, types of major customers, and distribution channels.
- *Industry and competition.* This covers an analysis of the industry or industries in which the organization is primarily situated. It examines the number and types of competitors, their share of the market, their marketing and production capabilities, their pricing postures, and other related factors.
- *Technology.* Included here is an analysis of the likely impact of related technology, both present and future, on the organization. Among other things, it addresses state-of-the-art developments, technical obsolescence, new applications, and product simplification trends.

### Internal Environment

- *CEO assessment of internal strengths and limitations.* The CEO once again presents a personal perspective on where the organization is especially strong or where sig-

nificant improvement is needed in strategically important areas, such as technical staff, sales staff, product
quality, production capacity, and image in the marketplace.

• *Financial.* This includes both past financial performance and future financial requirements for support of
the strategic plan, including both capital and operating
needs and alternatives available for the securing of appropriate funding.

• *Products/Services.* Both present and potential product
lines and/or service categories are identified here. These
need to be compatible with the data generated in the
various categories in external analysis.

• *Internal capabilities.* These would include an identification of both present and potential functions in such
areas as manufacturing, engineering, research and development, management information systems, marketing, and human resources.

These eight areas provide a basis for the detailed
structuring of specific analysis assignments. The following
questions need to be tailored to each individual organization as analysis formats are being structured in each of the
eight areas.

1.  Based on the mission statement, what are the key factors to be considered in this particular area? For example: When the mission statement includes product
development, then data on new products need to be
gathered as part of the products/services area on the
situation analysis wheel.

2.  What quantitative data are available and/or needed to
validate a particular issue? For example: When a preliminary critical issue concerns the technological obsolescence of a particular process, what is the dollar
impact on the organization?

3.  What trends have emerged over the last three to five
years? For example: "New products have averaged less

than 5 percent of total sales over the last three years;
obsolescence rate of existing products has exceeded
10 percent over the past three years."
4.   What are the future performance requirements for the
next three to five years? For example: "A minimum of
15 percent of sales must be in new products each year."
5.   What is the size of the gap between our past/present
performance and our future requirements? For example: "A minimum of 10 percent additional growth in
new product sales must be achieved each year."
6.   Do any of these issues need to be addressed immedi-
ately? During the strategic planning process, short-
term issues may be identified that require immediate
action. If so, specific assignments should be made,
even though they will not be a part of the strategic
analysis.

*Step 3. Completion of Analysis Assignments.* This is
an excellent opportunity for utilizing both line and staff
executives in strategic thinking and analysis. Generally, assignments are made on the basis of functional responsibility and experience. For example, the marketing vice president normally undertakes the market analysis, and the
chief financial officer is responsible for the financial analysis. However, if an individual on the planning team has a
strong conviction concerning a particular issue, this is an
opportunity for that person to do an in-depth analysis in
that area.

This is also a good time to bring in other members
of the organization who may not be on the planning team
but can make a valuable contribution. Although responsibility for analysis assignments still lies with the various
members of the team, they can delegate certain aspects of
their assignments.

One of the problems with strategic planning has
been an over-reliance on analytical tools. Many organizations have based their entire future direction on one analy-

sis technique. For example, the attention given to portfolio analysis in the 1970s periodically resulted in premature application of terms such as *cash cows, stars,* and *dogs* to business units that deserved a more in-depth analysis. This is not sound strategic planning. Our approach emphasizes the importance of the analysis being undertaken by operating managers. The utilization of various tools and techniques is based on the organization's ability to understand and apply them when and where needed. Four practical analysis techniques—gap analysis, the product-market matrix, portfolio analysis, and the life-cycle concept—are presented in the Resources section at the end of this book. Analytical tools such as these may be used when they strengthen the analysis or provide new insight.

An effective approach in this step is to do an in-depth analysis regarding the root causes behind the issues that have been determined to be the truly critical ones facing the organization. Additional facts are needed to analyze the root causes and develop alternatives to resolve these issues. It may be appropriate to form analysis teams at this time. These teams may include key line or staff people who are not members of the planning team but who have expertise in the particular analysis area. They may also include other members of the planning team who might present a broader perspective. For example, an analysis team examining new product opportunities might include representatives from marketing, finance, and production in order to provide a more comprehensive summary.

This critical-issue analysis consists of the following steps:

1. A narrative description and discussion of the issue, including why it is critical. When quantitative data are available to highlight the issue or show its impact on the organization, they should be included here.
2. An outline or analysis of the root causes, including evidence as to why they are root causes.

3.   A summary of broad-based conclusions, recommendations, and alternatives that exist for resolving this critical issue.

Two examples of critical-issue analysis, as it might
relate to a specific company, are shown in Figure 4.3.

*Step 4. Presentation of Analysis Assignments.* All
members of the planning team make formal presentations
of their findings and conclusions to the team. This method
of analysis presentation provides an excellent discipline for
communicating the issues and conclusions in a clear and
concise fashion.

Strategic analysis presentations should be limited to
three pages or less. This forces the individuals involved to
adopt a strategic summary point of view. Backup data can
be used as support material. Individual presentations tend
to be more productive when the major conclusions are
stated at the beginning in narrative form. Depending on
the type of analysis being presented, certain assignments
lend themselves more to a narrative form whereas others
need to have a statistical or quantitative approach. Basic
concepts or ideas require a narrative presentation; data
supporting certain conclusions or forecasting future trends
are communicated more effectively in a statistical format.
For example, in the case of future market growth (considered in the sample marketing analysis format presented in
Figure 4.4), a narrative analysis might include a descriptive
listing of potential markets along with the rationale for
pursuing them. Projected unit and dollar sales volume in
the same presentation would be the statistical data required to support the narrative analysis.

Some of the things to look for at the team presentation and discussion of analysis assignments are:

•  *Consistencies among various areas of the situation analysis wheel.* For example: "Market analysis concludes
that an increase in new product sales is needed to pene-

Figure 4.3. Two Examples of Critical Issue Analysis.

*Issue 1: Profitability Gap*

Critical Issue:

Significant profitability gap requires substantial increase in new product sales.

Supporting Data:

Real market growth rate for current products is projected at 2 to 3% per year for the next three years.

Growth rates for current products will level off and decline beginning in year four.

Profitability projections require a 15% annual sales increase in new products.

Root Causes:

Market research has been insufficient to identify viable new product opportunities.

Manufacturing capability is insufficient to produce required new products.

Conclusions:

Need a new product focus that will take advantage of our current strong sales channel via independent distributors.

Need new products that are compatible with our current manufacturing facilities.

Financial resources are not available for new plant or equipment.

*Issue 2: Competitive Price Pressures*

Critical Issue:

Inability to meet price pressures from competition.

Supporting Data:

Decline in gross profit margins from 30% to 24% during the last three years.

Decline in sales of 6% during the last three years.

Increase in labor cost of 15% during the last three years.

Root Causes:

Labor productivity has increased 2% per year while labor costs increased 5% per year.

Competitor A's productivity has increased 5% per year during same period.

Conclusions:

We need to achieve a minimum labor productivity rate increase of 5% per year. This productivity increase needs to occur with existing plant and equipment resources.

Figure 4.4. Sample Marketing Analysis Format.

*Strategic Marketing Analysis*

A.. Major conclusions (narrative)
   1. Future market growth
   2. Future market share
   3. Future market mix
B.  Actual results compared to plan—last three years (statistical)
   1. Unit and dollar sales volume
   2. Market share
   3. Market mix
C.  Actual results compared to plan—current year (statistical)
   1. Unit and dollar sales volume
   2. Market share
   3. Market mix
D.  Projections—next three years (statistical)
   1. Unit and dollar sales volume
   2. Market share
   3. Market mix
E.  Organization requirements to meet projections (narrative and statistical)

trate certain market segments. This is supported by financial analysis that shows that more new product sales are required to meet profitability targets."

- *Inconsistencies between various analysis areas.* For example: "R&D is investing heavily in new product development, but manufacturing has not projected sufficient capacity for producing these new products."

- *Confirmation of critical issues with tangible facts.* For example: "Expanded new product sales will require a substantial increase in the number of qualified applications engineers. Human resource analysis confirms a severe shortage of these engineers both internally and in the current labor market."

- *Identification of information gaps that require additional analysis.* For example: "There is insufficient information presented regarding new market growth opportunities."

*Step 5. Agreement on Analysis and Conclusions.* The team needs to reach agreement on the approach taken to analyze a particular area, the validity or credibility of the information presented, and the conclusions reached in each analysis area. This also should include agreement and prioritization of those two or three issues considered most critical. When certain analysis areas are incomplete, a partial repeat of the analysis may be necessary.

It is important for the team to reach agreement on the root causes of, and the major conclusions regarding, critical issues. These conclusions provide the basis for decisions and actions required to set strategy and determine long-term objectives.

Completing the strategic analysis, with no repeated analyses, may require two to four days of team meetings. Another two days may be required for team members to complete their individual assignments and prepare formal presentations. Teams embarking on strategic planning for the first time will probably require at least one partially repeated analysis. As the team gains experience with the analysis process, this approach may require less time. As indicated at the beginning of this chapter, strategic analysis requires a considerable amount of time to both prepare and present the analysis assignments. However, this is a sound investment of executive time, because this analysis is required to effectively define the organization's strategy, long-term objectives, and integrated programs. These important strategic decisions need to be based on a comprehensive assessment of both the external and internal environments of the organization.

## Why Does This Approach to Strategic Analysis Work?

Because this analysis approach involves the CEO and the planning team in doing their own analysis, and because a coach/facilitator helps identify and structure the analysis assignment but does not carry it out, the process is structured to ensure an analysis that is as complete as possible, even with an inexperienced team. Team presentations and discussions provide a series of checkpoints. There is a built-in provision for repeating portions of incomplete individual assignments. The two-phase approach of critical-issues agreement followed by structured analysis assignments, ensures a comprehensive and complete effort.

This analysis approach makes sense to the team because the initial focus is on broad-based critical issues. The CEO and the planning team usually have an intuitive feel for the critical issues facing their organization. CEOs, in particular, keep abreast of new industry trends, the potential impact of technology, new markets, and the like. Strategic analysis enables the team to utilize a systematic method or framework to check out their concepts and their beliefs about the future.

The exciting thing about this process is that the team creates its own strategic analysis. They experience firsthand what it takes to gather data, structure it, present it in a formal setting, answer questions about it, revise it, and draw conclusions. The analysis has tremendous credibility because it was developed by the team members themselves.

Each time this approach is used, new insights, new ways of thinking, and new ideas emerge. It is an excellent methodology for immersing executives and managers in the process of strategic thinking. They learn by doing. They utilize the information resources at their own disposal. They are required to defend their positions in front of their peers. And most important, they believe, and are committed to, the major conclusions coming out of the analysis because they formulated them.

A word of caution: There is a potential danger of getting into what is sometimes referred to as paralysis by analysis. Although completion of a certain amount of analysis is essential to any strategic plan, limits must be established. Determining a strict timetable and adhering to it is an effective way of preventing strategic analysis from unduly delaying completion of the plan itself.

## In Summary

Strategic analysis provides the data base from which subsequent strategic decisions are made. It begins with identification of external and internal critical issues that affect the organization's future. From that, supporting data are generated, root causes are pinpointed, and major conclusions regarding future action are reached. In addition to the important information shared, this approach provides an opportunity for planning-team members to get deeply involved in their own analysis and to gain further insight into the way other team members and their functions fit together. From this point, a determination of the organization's strategy, long-term objectives, and integrated programs becomes much more realistic.

# 5

# Formulating Strategy: Determining the Organization's Direction

Strategy, as was pointed out in Chapter One, addresses the *where* dimension of strategic planning rather than the *how*. Consequently, it comes after organization mission and strategic analysis but before long-term objectives. Although this may be different from your prior perceptions of strategy, this distinction will become clearer as this chapter develops.

**What Is Strategy?**

Strategy determines the overall direction of the organization. It requires the CEO and the planning team to think strategically in terms of *where* the organization should be going rather than *how* it should get there. Tregoe and Zimmerman (1980) have done a great deal to clarify the area of strategy, and their book, *Top Management Strategy: What It Is and How to Make It Work,* is recommended additional reading.

First of all, we would like to clearly differentiate between strategy formulation and long-range planning. Although long-range planning (long-term objectives and integrated programs) evolves from the determination of strategy, they are not the same. When long-range planning is done without putting effort into clearly determining an appropriate strategy, it tends to be largely an extrapolation of what has gone on in the past. This frequently results in managers making decisions based on operational rather than strategic perspectives. To quote Tregoe and Zimmerman, "The operations palliative, if taken alone, is dangerous medicine for treating a crisis or change which could threaten the survival of the business. If an organization is headed in the wrong direction, the last thing it needs is to get there more efficiently. And if an organization is headed in the right direction, it surely does not need to have that direction unwittingly changed by operational action taken in a strategic void" (p. 19).

Strategy determines the direction in which the organization needs to move to fulfill its mission. Experience has shown that it is important to go through strategic analysis prior to the formulation of strategy. Much of the data gathered in the analysis and many of the major conclusions reached will provide stimulus to the strategic thinking that must take place. As you go through this strategic-thinking process, it may cause you to go back and re-evaluate your statement of mission and perhaps make some modifications.

This chapter provides a specific approach for determining (or confirming) your organization's strategy. It includes:

1. defining and determining the discrete strategic areas that affect the direction of the organization
2. establishing these areas in priority order
3. determining the organization's driving force, both present and future
4. identifying changes that must take place if a new direction is indicated
5. formulating a strategy statement that establishes the clear direction of the organization

## What Are Strategic Areas?

Strategic areas represent major factors that decisively affect and influence the direction of the organization.

Tregoe and Zimmerman (pp. 45–53) identify nine basic strategic areas, some, or all, of which apply to every organization. The list that follows consists of their nine areas, to which we have added two more—services offered and customer needs—that some of our clients have found useful in describing their businesses. You may find it desirable to add to or modify some of these eleven areas so they clearly relate to your organization. Tregoe and Zimmerman's areas, and their definitions, are in quotes.*

1.  *"Products Offered.* Products are whatever an organization offers to the markets it serves, including ongoing support and maintenance. A product may be defined individually or as a line or grouping of products or subproducts. Products are defined on the basis of common characteristics such as functions performed, customer needs satisfied, size or form, durability, etc."

2.  *Services Offered.* Services represent those principal deliverables to the organization's customers that are primarily human effort including, but not limited to, such things as financial services, information services, medical and legal services, repair and maintenance, training, and the like. Products provided, if any, are incidental to the services rendered.

3.  *"Market Needs.* A market is a group of current or potential buyers or end users who share common needs. Market groupings could be formed on the basis of age, income, sex, education, ethnic background, occupation, industry, etc. These groupings may be formed or limited geographically."

4.  *Customer Needs.* Customer needs are differentiated from market needs when there is a predetermined group of users (individuals or organizations) and

---

*Quoted passages are used by permission of Kepner-Tregoe, Inc., a firm specializing in strategic and operational decision making, based in Princeton, N.J.

where expansion of the customer base is very limited, such as with a utility. Business expansion is dependent largely on increasing sales of, or adding new, deliverable products and services in response to the needs of that particular customer base.

5.  *"Technology.* A technology is a learned body of knowledge which is reproducible and subject to frequent update and extension. This would include the skills and knowledge possessed by those within the discipline, science or profession involved. It also includes the necessary systems, equipment and support facilities such as laboratories, libraries, and the like."

6.  *"Production Capability.* Production capability includes the production know-how, processes, systems and equipment required to make specific products, and the capability to improve those processes. In a service organization, the production capability includes those processes and skills required to provide the service(s) and any necessary support materials, procedures, programs, etc."

7.  *"Method of Sale.* The method of sale is the *primary* way an organization convinces current or potential customers or users to buy its products. This method of sale may be directed to both its customer and the end user (if different from its customer). This primary method of sale may be supported in a number of ways, such as advertising, display, direct mail, etc."

8.  *"Method of Distribution.* The method of distribution is the way products reach the customer, including field or in-route storage. This includes significant knowhow, systems and equipment to support the method of distribution. This *does not* include how the potential customer is persuaded to buy the product. For example, a rack display would be part of the method of sale. The method of distribution may be directed to both the customer and the end user (if different from the customer)."

9. *"Natural Resources.* Natural resources are those actual and potential forms of wealth supplied by nature. These would include coal, oil, metals, wood, water, usable land, etc. They would not include human resources or resources produced by people, such as money, processed foodstuffs, etc."

10. *"Size/Growth.* The size/growth of an organization is defined as its overall size and/or rate of growth as measured by the most appropriate indexes. For some organizations, size is most important and rate of growth is how it gets there. For other organizations, rate of growth is most important and size is only the result."

11. *"Return/Profit.* Return/profit is the financial result of an organization's effort. This result may be measured in a variety of ways, such as a percent of sales, return on assets or return on equity. In nonprofit organizations, measures of return may be in terms of cost/benefit ratio, budgetary control, or in quality or degree of services rendered."

It is important that the explanation of each strategic area be clearly understood. It will be helpful for the planning team to discuss each of these areas thoroughly enough that team members become comfortable with them and confident of their meanings and implications. Incorporating specific product/service or market examples from the organization's own experience into such discussions often helps facilitate this understanding.

## What Is the Driving Force?

The concept of the driving force, as espoused by Tregoe and Zimmerman, has made a major contribution to strategy formulation. They define the driving force as "the primary determiner of the scope of future products and markets" (p. 40). They also state that "all nine areas are critically important to every company. However, in every one of the organizations with which we have worked, we have found that *one and only one* of the . . . nine areas should be the Driving Force for the total organization" (p. 43). Other areas may represent important considerations, but "the ultimate question is: When the final decision about a product or market is made, which of these Strategic Areas proves to be the most decisive? This is the Driving Force" (p. 44).

Many organizations start out believing that return/ profit is their driving force. Our experience indicates that this is seldom true. Although virtually every organization in the private sector has a return/profit motive that clearly affects its decisions, it seldom is the primary factor on which future product/service/market decisions are made. Almost always, one or more of the other areas receives higher consideration. A major mental barrier for many senior executives to overcome is the acceptance that, although return/profit is vital to the survival of the organization, it is not necessarily the driving force. Acceptance of this fact opens up a whole new realm of thinking about strategy. This potential conflict can be addressed by acknowledging up front that achieving a reasonable return or profit is an absolute requirement even though one or more of the other strategic areas may impact future decisions more directly. Suggesting that return/profit, or any other strategic area, is not the driving force is not relegating it to a position of unimportance. It is merely placing that area in proper perspective with the others.

### How Are Priorities Established for Strategic Areas?

In preparation for this step, the planning team needs to reach consensus on exactly what the strategic areas are that affect the future direction of the organization. As mentioned, there needs to be sufficient discussion among team members to ensure complete understanding of what each strategic area represents. Use the definitions on pages 58 to 60 for reference. Each team member identifies the strategic areas that are relevant to the organization and places them in priority order, prior to the planning meeting. This encourages individuals to think in terms of their own perspectives before sharing them with others.

At the meeting, the coach/facilitator guides the group to an agreement on the strategic areas relevant to that organization. Then the coach/facilitator uses the decision matrix (see Figure 5.1) to help the team draw comparisons between each strategic area and each of the others to determine the relative importance of the areas. It is essential that the criteria for choosing one strategic area over another be based on which area has the greater effect on determining the scope of *future* products/services and markets. Application of these criteria must be consistent while the team is comparing one area with another.

The discussions that take place as each area is compared with each of the others are quite revealing in terms of the ways various team members view how future product/service/market decisions should be made. The liveliest discussions frequently come when comparing return/profit with other areas.

The key value in using the decision matrix is that a clear decision must be reached when comparing two specific areas. They cannot be declared of equal value. Frequently, one of the surprising discoveries comes when an organization that considers itself to be customer oriented finds that its number one priority is products offered rather than market needs. Incidentally, it is quite consistent to have an organization that has products offered as its top priority and that also places a high value on being customer oriented.

Upon completion of the decision matrix by the team, there should be a clear priority ranking of the number one strategic area followed by numbers two, three, and so on. The number one area then becomes the driving force for the organization, and a strategy statement is developed around this driving force. Figure 5.2 is an example of a completed decision matrix in which technology emerges as the driving force.

Figure 5.1. Strategic Areas Decision Matrix.

| | 1 | 2 | 3 | 4 | 5 | 6 | 7 | 8 | 9 | 10 | 11 | 12 | 13 | 14 | TOTAL X's | |
|---|---|---|---|---|---|---|---|---|---|---|---|---|---|---|---|---|
| | Products Offered | Services Offered | Market Needs | Customer Needs | Technology | Production Capability | Method of Sale | Method of Distribution | Natural Resources | Size/Growth | Return/Profit | | | | | |
| Products Offered | | | | | | | | | | | | | | | | 1 |
| Services Offered | | | | | | | | | | | | | | | | 2 |
| Market Needs | | | | | | | | | | | | | | | | 3 |
| Customer Needs | | | | | | | | | | | | | | | | 4 |
| Technology | | | | | | | | | | | | | | | | 5 |
| Production Capability | | | | | | | | | | | | | | | | 6 |
| Method of Sale | | | | | | | | | | | | | | | | 7 |
| Method of Distribution | | | | | | | | | | | | | | | | 8 |
| Natural Resources | | | | | | | | | | | | | | | | 9 |
| Size/Growth | | | | | | | | | | | | | | | | 10 |
| Return/Profit | | | | | | | | | | | | | | | | 11 |
| | | | | | | | | | | | | | | | | 12 |
| | | | | | | | | | | | | | | | | 13 |
| | | | | | | | | | | | | | | | | 14 |
| | 1 | 2 | 3 | 4 | 5 | 6 | 7 | 8 | 9 | 10 | 11 | 12 | 13 | 14 | | |
| Vertical (spaces) | | | | | | | | | | | | | | | | |
| Horizontal (X's) | | | | | | | | | | | | | | | | |
| TOTAL | | | | | | | | | | | | | | | | |
| Rank Order | | | | | | | | | | | | | | | | |

*Instructions*

Review list of strategic areas and eliminate any that do not apply to your organization; add any additional ones that may be appropriate on the blank lines, repeating each under the corresponding number at the top.

Evaluate #1 against #2. If *more important*, place x in box under #2; if *less important*, leave blank. Repeat with *each* remaining number. Continue to next line; repeat.

Total x's across for each number; enter in "Horizontal" box at bottom; total spaces down for each number; enter in "Vertical" box at bottom; *add both* for TOTAL.

Largest number under "TOTAL" will be 1 in "Rank Order"; next largest will be 2, and so on. If two or more areas have same total, rank order is determined by comparing each subjectively against others with the same total.

urce: Copyright © George L. Morrisey, 1974.

Figure 5.2. Example of Completed Decision Matrix.

| | 1 Products Offered | 2 Services Offered | 3 Market Needs | 4 Customer Needs | 5 Technology | 6 Production Capability | 7 Method of Sale | 8 Method of Distribution | 9 Natural Resources | 10 Size/Growth | 11 Return/Profit | 12 | 13 | 14 | TOTAL X's |
|---|---|---|---|---|---|---|---|---|---|---|---|---|---|---|---|
| 1 Products Offered | | X | | | | | X | X | | | | | | | 3 |
| 2 Services Offered | | | | | | | X | X | | | | | | | 2 |
| 3 Market Needs | | | | X | | X | X | X | | X | X | | | | 6 |
| 4 Customer Needs | | | | | | | X | X | | X | X | | | | 4 |
| 5 Technology | | | | | | X | X | X | | X | X | | | | 5 |
| 6 Production Capability | | | | | | | X | X | | X | X | | | | 4 |
| 7 Method of Sale | | | | | | | | X | | | | | | | 1 |
| 8 Method of Distribution | | | | | | | | | | | | | | | 0 |
| 9 Natural Resources | | | | | | | | | | | | | | | NOT RELEVANT |
| 10 Size/Growth | | | | | | | | | | | | | | | 0 |
| 11 Return/Profit | | | | | | | | | | | | | | | 0 |
| 12 | | | | | | | | | | | | | | | |
| 13 | | | | | | | | | | | | | | | |
| 14 | | | | | | | | | | | | | | | |

| | 1 | 2 | 3 | 4 | 5 | 6 | 7 | 8 | 9 | 10 | 11 | 12 | 13 | 14 |
|---|---|---|---|---|---|---|---|---|---|---|---|---|---|---|
| Vertical (spaces) | 0 | 0 | 2 | 2 | 4 | 3 | 0 | 0 | | 4 | 5 | | | |
| Horizontal (X's) | 3 | 2 | 6 | 4 | 5 | 4 | 1 | 0 | | 0 | 0 | | | |
| TOTAL | 3 | 2 | 8 | 6 | 9 | 7 | 1 | 0 | | 4 | 5 | | | |
| Rank Order | 7 | 8 | 2 | 4 | 1 | 3 | 9 | 10 | | 6 | 5 | | | |

Another valuable use of the decision matrix approach is to maintain visibility on the second- and third-ranked strategic areas. They are also important and will serve as potential sources for long-term objectives. For example, an organization with a market-needs driving force might have method of distribution as its number-two area. This may call for a long-term objective related to expanding the distribution system in order to respond more quickly to identified market needs.

At this point, it may be desirable to stop and check on the compatibility between the types of critical issues determined and conclusions reached in the strategic analysis section and the priority strategic areas selected via the decision matrix. For example, if products offered is selected as the driving force, yet the major strategic issue facing the organization is the need to diversify the business into unrelated product areas in order to offset the cyclical nature of the business, there is a potential conflict or incompatibility between the driving force (or strategy) and the most critical long-term issue facing the organization. Before proceeding, this incompatibility needs to be resolved. A products-offered strategy maintains that new products will be similar to existing products. This is not compatible with a need to diversify products outside of the current product line to offset potential cyclical declines or strengthen the overall product-market mix.

## How Is a Strategy Statement Developed?

A strategy statement is developed by answering five fundamental questions:

1.  What should be our future driving force?
2.  How does this differ from our current driving force?
3.  What changes will be needed to meet the requirements of our future driving force?
4.  How is this compatible with our mission?
5.  How is this compatible with the conclusions from our strategic analysis?

Until now, the discussions have led the team to focus on the organization's future direction. Is there a clear driving force that all can accept or, as is more frequently the case, is there a fragmented approach in which different strategic areas dominate, depending on the circumstances? Strategy discussions at the executive level anticipate and encourage differences. This is one reason why the coach/facilitator needs to be someone without a vested interest in the outcome. Differences, expressed in a constructive manner, result in better definition of the organization's future direction. Ideally, the planning team reaches a consensus on what the total organization's driving force will be in the future. However, recognizing that the planning team is really an extension of the office of the CEO, when a consensus appears impossible, the CEO may have to make the decision.

The planning team next determines the organization's current direction. If there is no agreement on the current driving force, the coach/facilitator may have to lead the team through another consensus exercise. A common viewpoint of the organization's current strategy is just as important as determining its future strategy.

With the differences clearly in mind, the planning team can normally identify the major changes that need to take place. If not, some further analysis may be required.

For example, a major division of a well-known company in the telecommunications field had for years been in a services-offered mode largely based on the fact that much of its business was in a regulated environment. However, with the advent of deregulation of the telephone industry, the company recognized that it must move to a customer-needs emphasis if it were to survive and grow.

Consequently, their statement of strategy is "We intend to move from a services-offered to a customer-needs strategy. The primary reasons are to offset the impact of new competition brought about by deregulation and to meet the financial commitments established in the company's mission. For this to happen, the following changes need to take place:

- more product diversification related to customer needs
- strong internal focus on employee attitudes, training, and broadening of capabilities to meet the customer-needs posture
- more accurate analysis of profitability, by customer groupings
- organizational change to reflect customer needs posture
- company image enhancement as a customer-needs-driven organization
- improved definition of customer service requirements"

Having reached these conclusions, the company was in a position to set long-term objectives and implement related integrated programs to bring these changes about.

The process of strategic planning in general and strategy formulation in particular has to take place in an atmosphere where creative thinking is encouraged. The planning team has to approach the strategy setting session with an eye toward what we would like to be rather than what we are. The role of the coach/facilitator is especially critical in these discussions to make sure that no initial restraints are placed on any creative ideas that may flow. Frequently, seemingly impractical concepts can be modified to make them feasible or can trigger other ideas that might not have come up otherwise. Remember, the purpose of the strategy statement is to clarify and outline the *future* direction of the organization.

## In Summary

Strategy determines the direction of the organization rather than its destination or methodology (which are operational). It requires fresh thinking in a no-holds-barred atmosphere to make certain that the future is more than a carbon copy of the past. It includes identification of relevant strategic areas; determination of the driving force, both current and in the future; and formulation of a statement that clearly identifies where the organization should be headed. Organizational strategy needs to be formally reviewed annually or at any other time there is a major change that affects the organization's business. With a clear statement of strategy that supports the organization's mission and is compatible with the conclusions reached in strategic analysis, you are now ready to proceed with setting long-term objectives.

# 6

 Selecting and
Validating Long-Term
Objectives

## What Are Long-Term Objectives?

Long-term objectives describe what the organization wants to have or become at some point in the future, usually within three to five years. Although these objectives must have a degree of measurability, they will differ considerably from annual operational objectives. (Operational objectives are considerably more precise and will be covered in substantial detail in Volume Two of this series.) Because long-term objectives are strategic in nature, they focus more on a position to be attained than on specific accomplishments. As you do your subsequent operational planning, a series of specific results need to be identified in order to achieve the desired position. For example, a long-term objective for a service-related company might be "to become the dominant supplier of [designated] services to [designated] market segments." Naturally, for this to happen, a series of specific accomplishments related to such things as service type and quality, market penetration, and resource acquisition and allocation, as well as a definition of *dominant*, must be established along the way as a part of the operational plan.

Although financial projections (covered in Chapter

Eight) are also a part of long-term objectives, they tend to be quite different in our strategic planning model. In the past, financial projections have frequently been an extrapolation from where the organization is now. Long-term objectives, on the other hand, tend to work in reverse. They identify where you want to be at a point in the future and then work backward to the present in order to determine interim steps along the way.

### Where Do Long-Term Objectives Originate?

The first step is to review the mission, analysis, and strategy. Out of these three will flow those categories within which long-term objectives must be set. Prior to setting long-term objectives, there must be a clear distinction between strategic and operational categories. For example, a need to change the organization's driving force would be strategic in nature whereas acquiring the necessary personnel to support that change would be operational. Although it may be necessary to identify specific operational factors that need to be addressed, those factors should be considered at a separate time. The important first step is to identify those three to six strategic categories within which objectives need to be set.

### How Are Long-Term Objectives Selected?

Long-term objectives are selected at a team planning meeting. The following process, all or in part, may be used:

1. Identify strategic categories that need to be considered for potential long-term objectives. Determine which are the three to six most important.
2. Identify, within each category, the potential results that will move the organization closer to its mission and strategy. These results should be broad in scope and highly visionary.

3. Select and reach consensus on the three to six long-term objectives. Where possible, write them in an objectives format: "To have (or become) [*the result*] by [*year*] ."

Although there may be more than three to six long-term objectives that are important to the organization's future, those chosen should represent the critical few that will provide the greatest contribution toward carrying out the mission and strategy. They should come as a result of team consensus. Additional objectives considered worthy may be assigned to specific departments or units.

## What Are Some Examples of Long-Term Objectives?

As indicated earlier, there is a distinction between financial projections and long-term objectives. Long-term objectives represent what the organization wants to have or become at some point in the future. Some potential strategic categories within which long-term objectives may be set, together with some examples of each, are listed in Figure 6.1.

## How Are Long-Term Objectives Validated?

Long-term objectives generally start out as preliminary statements of what you want to have or become. They may be based largely on your desires rather than your assurance that they can be accomplished. Therefore, you need to check each statement against some or all of the following criteria:

1. *Is it measurable or verifiable?* Will you and others affected be able to recognize it when it happens? For example, an objective statement like "to become the dominant supplier" needs to be measured by market share or other similar indicators. Also, information on the competition must be readily available.

Figure 6.1. Examples of Long-Term Objectives.

| Strategic Category | Long-Term Objective |
|---|---|
| Market position | To become the dominant supplier of [designated] services to [designated] market segments by [year]. |
| New markets | To have at least 20% of revenue in [year] from markets not currently being served. |
| Product/service mix | To have a minimum of 20% of sales from new products (or services) by [year]. |
| Technology | To have a separate research capability in [technology] by [year]. |
| Human resources | To have an Integrated Planning Process involving all employees in the organization by [year]. |
| Image | To become recognized as one of the top three companies in our industry in terms of service by [year]. |
| Growth/diversification | To become a multinational corporation with a minimum of 30% of net revenue coming from foreign sources by [year]. |
| Profitability | To have all mature product lines producing a minimum net profit of [percentage] of sales by [year]. |

2. *Is it achievable or feasible?* There is no point in establishing an objective that is clearly beyond reach. What major efforts or significant changes must take place in order to achieve the objective? What is the likelihood of these happening? To answer these questions may require addressing such issues as human capabilities, financial resources, other priorities, impact of competition, or outside influences. It may be that the integrated program for that objective needs to be developed before you can fully determine whether that objective is feasible or achievable.

3. *Is it flexible or adaptable?* Because there are a number of unknown factors, whatever objective you set must be flexible enough to take into account changing circumstances and new related opportunities. For exam-

ple, what you establish as a five-year objective may not necessarily be what is accomplished during that five-year period. As you go through the annual process of updating the strategic plan, the objective may need to be modified to reflect up-to-date information.

4. *Is it consistent with the rest of the plan?* Does this objective move you closer to the positions that have been taken as you constructed your mission, strategic analysis, and strategy?

### Where Do Assumptions Fit in the Planning Process?

The analysis section of many strategic plans includes assumptions. However, we believe assumptions more appropriately belong with long-term objectives. These objectives may be based on assumptions over which the organization has little or no control. For example, the objective "to become the dominant supplier" might be based on such assumptions as:

- There will be a continuing need for those services in those market segments as projected by industry statistics.
- There will be no major technological changes in the industry that could obsolete the need for those services.

When long-term objectives are based on assumptions, these assumptions should be included as a part of the plan along with the objectives. When assumptions change, the objectives must be re-examined and may have to be revised in the light of new information.

### In Summary

Long-term objectives derive from the mission, analysis, and strategy and describe what the organization wants to have or become at some point in the future. Normally, three to six long-term objectives are appropriate for most organizations. More than that tend to diffuse the organization's focus, which needs to be on those specific accomplishments that will lead the organization closer to carrying out its mission and strategy. Once agreed to by the planning team, long-term objectives provide the basis for moving into integrated programs where accountability for specific results needs to be established.

# 7

Translating
Ideas into Action
Through Integrated
Programs

## What Are Integrated Programs?

Integrated programs are the action steps of strategic planning. They become integrated because of the cross-functional nature of these programs. This is the first time that ideas get translated into specific actions. This is also the first time that strategy and long-term objectives really get tested. It is the crunch point in strategic planning. Is the plan realistic? Will it work? Are there the know-how and resources to make it happen? Who will be held accountable for specific results? All of these questions are answered in the integrated programs section of the strategic plan.

At this point in the strategic planning process, it is important that organizational integration becomes a focal point for carrying out the strategy and accomplishing the long-term objectives. The term *integrated programs* has been carefully chosen because it reflects the true nature of this element. For example, an organization with a market-needs driving force is likely to have at least one long-term objective related to new market development. The type of program required to achieve that objective probably will involve substantial effort from marketing, sales, engineering, production, and finance if it is to succeed.

Another reason for using the word *integrated* here is that this is the element that provides the strongest bridge to the operational plan. Portions of the integrated programs will show up as short-term objectives in the operational plan.

Time and time again, the major difference between an average and a superior organization in the same industry is that the superior performer is continually working on two or three integrated programs that are critical to its long-term success. This frequently results in that organization being years ahead of its competition.

### What Is the Purpose of Integrated Programs?

The purpose of integrated programs is to ensure that the plan will be implemented. Integrated programs need to be laid out in enough detail for the CEO to track progress and measure results. There is no mystery in making this happen. Implementation revolves around making the translation from objectives into specific actions and results. Most organizations have difficulty making this translation because they do not have sufficiently detailed integrated programs or because their programs are written in vague generalities without a strong results focus. It takes considerable skill to keep the team continually focused on practical and realistic results. An experienced coach/facilitator can guide the team in translating ideas, issues, and concerns into specific results with a minimum of wheel-spinning.

### What Are Key Factors in Developing Integrated Programs?

The CEO plays a very strong leadership role in establishing and monitoring integrated programs. Although most of the effort is likely to be carried out by others, these programs turn out to be the CEO's personal action plans for achieving long-term objectives. Therefore, there must be sufficient detail to provide the visibility necessary for the CEO to be able to effectively monitor the programs and review results. This also requires the CEO to fix accountability to individual team members for each of the steps in these programs.

Developing integrated programs is an exciting aspect of strategic planning. It is action- and results-oriented. It continually forces the team to focus on specific and measurable organizational results. It is also exciting because, at this point, the team begins to see exactly how they are going to achieve their long-term objectives. Consequently, it enhances the credibility of both the process and the plan.

The CEO must make sure that managers are not overcommitting themselves or underestimating what will be required to accomplish long-term objectives. In addition to carrying out these programs, managers are still accountable for the operating results in their respective areas. Therefore, the number of long-term objectives to be translated into programs must be limited. Furthermore, each program should be limited to between five and ten major steps. Many things happen in an organization without the need for written detailed plans and programs. So, be very selective in the integrated programs you develop. Choose only those priority areas where formal planning is a necessity.

## How Are Integrated Programs Identified and Documented?

There are seven steps recommended for identifying and documenting integrated programs. These steps, which may be adapted to fit your requirements, are:

1.  Identify the results needed to accomplish each long-term objective. The focus of this step is on implementation and results (the decision has already been made regarding the specific long-term objectives to be pursued). The use of a brainstorming approach is an excel-

cellent way to get group participation and involvement and is also a good way to get all the implementation ideas out on the table. It is one of the quickest
ways to get an idea of how to approach the particular
objective. Specific questions that should be asked by
the coach/facilitator at this stage include:

    a. What are the key factors that need to be ad-
dressed in order to achieve this objective? (The
strategic analysis process has already brought
out the critical issues, root causes, and recommended alternatives, so don't re-invent the
wheel. Refer back to the analysis section; planning is an iterative process.)

    b. What specific results are needed to attain the
objective? More specifically, what results need
to be accomplished by the end of the first
quarter, the second quarter; by the end of the
first year, the second year, and so on?

    c. What feedback mechanisms are in place or are
needed to monitor progress toward these results? (At this point, pay particular attention
to controls already in place. Most organizations
have more information and reports than are
needed. Rather than add additional ones, this is
a good time to eliminate those that are un-
necessary.)

2. Select the five to ten most critical results required to
achieve the long-term objective. Specific questions
that should be answered include:

    a. What are the measurable results, and what are
the time frames for their completion?

    b. What are the specific actions or activities re-
quired to achieve each result? (Here the CEO
makes sure enough detail is spelled out so it is
possible to personally monitor progress and results.)

    c. Which specific individual in the organization is

accountable for each result? (If this individual is not an obvious choice, the CEO may need to make an assignment.)

d.  Is a detailed schedule needed to ensure that each result is achieved?

e.  What resources (such as people, capital, and time) are needed to make each result happen? Are those resources already available, or do you need to obtain them?

f.  What feedback mechanisms will be used to monitor progress?

3.  Agree on approach. Once each integrated program has been developed, the following questions are asked: Will this approach work? Is the program complete? Does it make sense? Can you afford it? Are there alternatives you have not considered? The CEO makes the final judgment in this area.

4.  For each integrated program, reach agreement on and document the results concerning the areas outlined in Figure 7.1. For an example of how this might be done, see Figure 7.2.

5.  Invite review by and comment from the levels of management that will be implementing these programs. This is an excellent opportunity to get the participation of others in the strategic planning process. Their involvement at this stage may be an important key to getting their commitment to the overall strategic plan when it is finished.

6.  Complete final documentation of the integrated programs. After the next level of management has been given a chance to review and comment on the integrated programs, a final group review is held with the CEO and the team. The result should be a final plan ready for implementation. However, integrated programs (or any plans for that matter) are never cast in concrete. They may be modified at any time when justified by changing circumstances.

Figure 7.1. Integrated Programs Format.

| Long-Term Objective: | | | | |
|---|---|---|---|---|
| Results | Timetable | Resources | Accountability | Feedback Mechanism |
| | | | | |

*Source: The Executive Guide to Strategic Planning* by Patrick J. Below, George L. Morrisey, and Betty L. Acomb. San Francisco: Jossey-Bass. Copyright © 1987. Permission to reproduce hereby granted.

Figure 7.2. Example of an Integrated Program.

| Long-Term Objective: | To have a minimum of 20% of our sales ($5.0MM in constant dollars) in new products by [year]. | | | |
|---|---|---|---|---|
| Results | Timetable | Resources | Accountability | Feedback Mechanism |
| 1. Complete market research to identify 3 new product opportunities. | Year 1, Quarter 1 | $ 30,000 | V-P Marketing | Market research report |
| 2. Complete product specifications and engineering design for products A and B. | Year 1, Quarter 2 | 2,000 hours | V-P Engineering | Product and engineering specifications |
| 3. Initiate manufacture of new products. | Year 1, Quarter 3 | 100 hours | V-P Manufacturing | Production plan |
| 4. Complete marketing plan for product A. | Year 1, Quarter 3 | 100 hours | V-P Marketing | Market plan |
| 5. First-year sales results for new products: $0.5MM. | Year 1, Quarter 4 | (part of existing sales program) | V-P Sales | Quarterly sales reports |
| 6. Complete marketing plan for product B. | Year 2, Quarter 1 | 100 hours | V-P Marketing | Market plan |
| 7. Finalize product specifications and engineering design for product C. | Year 2, Quarter 2 | 1,000 hours | V-P Engineering | Product and engineering specifications |
| 8. Complete marketing plan for product C. | Year 2, Quarter 3 | 100 hours | V-P Marketing | Market plan |
| 9. Second-year sales results for new products: $2.5MM. | Year 2 | (part of existing sales program) | V-P Sales | Quarterly sales reports |
| 10. Third-year sales results for new products: $5.0 MM. | Year 3 | $100,000 for new product advertising and promotion | V-P Sales | Quarterly sales reports |

7.   Implement and evaluate the programs. Each integrated program needs a solid starting point so those who are responsible for carrying out the related actions can proceed accordingly. Measurable results for each program should be structured for a quarterly review to ensure that the program is being implemented. It is far too easy for operating pressures to overshadow these programs. It is vitally important that the programs receive high visibility and support from the CEO and the planning team.

All integrated programs are reviewed in depth by the team each quarter. These reviews are one of top management's most important functions. The CEO leads the quarterly reviews. Written reports should be submitted in advance and presented orally at each meeting. Changes and revisions to integrated programs are made as appropriate.

## How Are Integrated Programs Linked with the Operational Plan?

The very nature of integrated programs is to identify specific results required, fix accountability, estimate resources, and establish timetables and feedback mechanisms. These aspects are very similar to certain operational planning techniques that will be described in the second book in this series. This forms a natural linkage between the strategic and operational plans.

The operational plan addresses both short-term (that is, the first year) requirements specified in the strategic plan, usually in the integrated-programs section, and current operating results. So it is not just a matter of translating all the integrated programs into more detailed operational plans. However, by clearly identifying these integrated programs before developing the operational plan, they can be more easily adapted to meet operating requirements. This results in an operational plan that focuses on both long-term strategic and short-term operational results.

## In Summary

Integrated programs identify and fix accountability for the specific actions and results required to accomplish long-term objectives. These are still broad in nature but provide the basis from which operational plans can be developed later. They are specific enough, however, to be sufficiently visible to the CEO and the planning team so it can be determined if their long-term objectives will be achieved.

# 8

# Compiling
# and Presenting
# Financial Projections

## Why Is There a Separate Financial Projections Section?

The financial projections section is where all related financial information is compiled and presented. For financial projections to be credible, the numbers must be consistent with the rest of the plan and must make sense to the team. Clear understanding of financial projections by the planning team is critical. However, this is not a detailed budget-level projection but rather an executive-level financial summary. The preceding sections of the plan—strategic analysis, strategy, long-term objectives, and integrated programs—should lead to financial projections that are realistic and acceptable to the team and to other groups who may be receiving and/or approving the plan. The financial projections section is the financial summation of the plan. Its purpose is:

1.  to present the planned financial results
2.  to provide a format for financial communication and understanding
3.  to organize all finance-related information in one section of the plan

## What Is the Recommended Content?

Financial projections are structured to provide a comprehensive translation of the plan into financial terms. All financial projections should include:

1. a forecast income statement
2. a forecast balance sheet
3. a capital expenditures forecast
4. key indicators of financial performance (forecast)
5. a financial narrative summary

These projections should be in both current and constant dollars.

*Income Statement.* The income statement is structured in enough detail to be easily reviewed and analyzed by senior management. Sources of revenue are broken down according to meaningful categories that are strategically important to the company (for example, geography, markets, product lines, methods of distribution). Gross margin, operating expenses, and net income are expressed in both dollars and percentage of sales. This is an income statement that supports the projections of the plan rather than a detailed line item income statement. Figure 8.1 depicts a sample income statement for a set of individual product lines.

*Balance Sheet.* The balance sheet summarizes the financial makeup of the business in terms of where the capital comes from and how it is employed. It includes total organization information, such as the asset and liability structure, the debt-to-equity ratio, and inventory types and levels. This information summarizes the financial position and integrity of the organization at various points in time. See Figure 8.2 for a sample summary balance sheet.

Figure 8.1. Sample Income Statement.
(Expressed in 000s.)

| | Product Lines | | | |
| | 1 | 2 | 3 | Total |
|---|---|---|---|---|
| Sales (current) | $5,000 | $8,000 | $12,000 | $25,000 |
| Sales (constant) | $4,750 | $7,680 | $11,520 | $23,950 |
| Sales in units | 500 | 1,000 | 1,500 | 3,000 |
| Cost of sales | $3,500 | $5,000 | $ 9,000 | $17,500 |
| Gross margin | $1,500 | $3,000 | $ 3,000 | $ 7,500 |
| Gross margin (%) | 30.0 | 37.5 | 25.0 | 30.0 |
| Operating expenses | $1,500 | $2,000 | $ 2,000 | $ 5,500 |
| Operating expenses (%) | 30.0 | 25.0 | 16.6 | 22.0 |
| Net income | $ 0 | $1,000 | $ 1,000 | $ 2,000 |
| Net income (%) | 0 | 12.5 | 8.5 | 8.0 |

Figure 8.2. Sample Summary Balance Sheet.
(Expressed in 000s.)

*Assets:*

| | | |
|---|---|---|
| Cash | | $ 100 |
| Accounts receivable | | 150 |
| Inventory | | |
| — Raw materials | | 200 |
| — Work in process | | 200 |
| — Finished goods | | 800 |
| Property, plant and equipment | $2,500 | |
| Less accumulated depreciation | (500) | |
| Property, plant and equipment—Net | | 2,000 |
| Total assets | | $3,450 |

*Liabilities:*

| | |
|---|---|
| Accounts payable | $ 100 |
| Other current liabilities | 600 |
| Long-term debt | 700 |
| Equity | 2,050 |
| Total liabilities | $3,450 |

*Capital Expenditures Forecast.* Capital expenditure requirements for support of the long-term objectives and integrated programs must be spelled out. When there are capital expenditure requirements identified in the integrated programs, they need to be included in this list (for a sample list see Figure 8.3). For example, if new equipment is required to automate a particular product line, the specific investment level must be identified with that particular program. If exact investment numbers are not available, estimates or ranges are acceptable. The primary focus is agreement, in principle, on the approximate level of capital expenditures required to support the plan and on the appropriate rate of return on that capital. This will involve managers in selecting appropriate measures of rates of return that consider the time value of money.

Figure 8.3. Sample Capital Expenditures.
(Expressed in 000s.)

| Integrated Program | Capital Expenditure | Year | | | Amount |
| --- | --- | --- | --- | --- | --- |
| | | 1 | 2 | 3 | |
| Engineering | Engineering prototype lab | X | | | $350 |
| Manufacturing | New product line equipment | | X | | $250 |
| Distribution | Warehouse expansion | | | X | $125 |
| | | | | Total | $725 |

*Key Financial Indicators.* Key financial indicators are those senior management has selected as being of strategic importance in running their organization and for measuring performance against plan (some examples are listed in Figure 8.4). There are two usual methods for presenting these financial indicators—ratios and trends. They are both necessary. One method includes the indicators within the various financial statements. For example, in Figure 8.1, the gross margin percentage for each product line is included in the income statement. This provides immediate and complete information while reviewing the statement. The second method groups certain indicators in a separate category, as shown in Figure 8.4.

In order to assess the key financial indicators that

Figure 8.4. Sample Key Financial Indicators.

Return on invested capital
Return on total assets
Inventory turnover ratio
Debt-to-equity ratio
Earnings per share
Net sales per employee
Break-even point and margin of safety


have a major impact on an organization's financial performance as measured by return on investment (ROI), we
have included Figure 8.5. This figure should be used as a
guide to decide which key financial indicators to include in
the financial projections section of your strategic plan.

*Financial Narrative.* The financial narrative should
pull together the elements of price, volume, cost, and control, and communicate them in such a manner that their
interaction is clear to all managers. Financial projections
are more than numbers and ratios; there is also a financial
story to be told. The financial narrative is written by the
chief financial officer (CFO). Its purpose is to highlight the
key financial issues, concerns, and trends. For example,
when access to capital is a factor that will limit plan implementation, or when debt-to-equity ratio is a key financial
indicator in the plan, this information needs additional
commentary. In a similar vein, when financial issues are critical to understanding the plan, these issues should be sum-
marized and presented in narrative form. An example of
this might be the location of a substantial portion of an organization's assets in a foreign country that has widely
fluctuating exchange rates. Such an issue needs to be clearly spelled out in the financial projections section of the
plan. The financial narrative should also summarize the
major financial implications of the plan. For example: "Increase the equity by 50 percent, increase the asset base by
25 percent." Also, the financial assumptions on which the
plan is based should be made explicit.

Figure 8.5. Financial Model for Planning Return on Investment
(ROI).

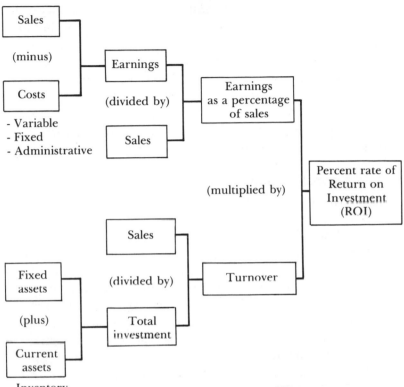

## Why Are Historic Financial Trends Necessary?

It is an excellent practice to include historic trends for all financial information because the history of past results, together with future projections may provide additional insight into the credibility of the forecasts. Thus, when a three-year forward projection of sales is included, a three-year past history of sales results should also be included.

## Who Compiles the Financial Projections?

The CFO (or equivalent) has the responsibility of compiling the financial projections. This individual should have an awareness of the type of financial information required by the CEO, the board of directors, or other interested parties. Consequently, the CFO decides the level of detail and the specific financial formats to be used. The information in the financial projections is then reviewed and discussed by team members, who help the CFO anticipate questions likely to be asked during presentation of the plan.

## How Are Higher-Level Financial Requirements Handled?

Many organizations are commonly required to provide others with financial information similar to that addressed in financial projections. Such information could be required by a parent company, holding company, senior corporate group, super agency or legislative group (in the case of governmental organizations), or by venture capitalists, to name a few possibilities. Frequently, this task involves the completion of a series of forms requiring specific financial information. Although this need clearly must be met, financial forms completion requirements should not drive the strategic planning process.

It is imperative that the planning team structure the financial projections section to meet their specific needs, not merely to be able to fill out the required financial forms. They have the responsibility for development and implementation of their own plan. They can do this most effectively by using the guidelines and recommendations presented in this chapter to develop financial projections that are relevant to their situation.

## In Summary

Financial projections pull together all the finance-related information into one place. The CFO (or equivalent) is responsible for summarizing all the financial data required to support the strategic plan. There is generally no new information generated here. The financial projections, together with the executive summary covered in the next chapter, provide an overview of the entire strategic plan.

# 9

# Preparing
# an Executive
# Summary

## What Is the Executive Summary?

The executive summary is the CEO's personal summation of, and commitment to, the strategic plan. It summarizes the plan, identifies the issues, tests the logic of the information presented, and pulls the plan sharply into focus. The executive summary is written using the style and management values of the CEO. It is consistent with, and supported by, the other sections of the plan. When writing this summary, the CEO integrates the various sections of the plan and gives them direction and a sense of cohesiveness.

It is important that the CEO devote sufficient time and effort to the writing of the executive summary. It may take several drafts before satisfaction is reached in terms of condensing the information, summarizing the content, communicating the CEO's philosophy clearly, and articulating the major challenges to implementation of the plan. However, it must be remembered that planning is the CEO's primary responsibility within the organization. The executive summary is the principal link between the CEO and the total organization for:

1.  communicating vision
2.  establishing priorities
3.  assisting in plan implementation
4.  demonstrating commitment to the plan

## Why Is the Executive Summary Needed?

The executive summary is one of the most powerful communication tools available to the CEO. It sets the stage and the tone for communication and implementation of the strategic plan. It should be widely circulated and carefully studied by the entire organization.

The executive summary is a direct reflection of the views of the leader of the organization. By putting these thoughts in writing, the CEO's vision is crystallized and validated along with the team's perception of that vision. If there are inconsistencies or misunderstandings between the CEO and members of the planning team, the executive summary will bring these differences to the surface. The result is a total commitment by the team regarding the plan.

The executive summary also provides an opportunity for articulation of the CEO's vision of the future, including the organization's mission, strategy, and long-term objectives. The more this vision is communicated and discussed, the more likely it is that a common vision will emerge and become internalized throughout the total organization. The executive summary thereby provides a key link between the strategic plan and the total organization in terms of developing understanding and generating belief in and commitment to the plan.

A third reason the executive summary is needed is that it is an essential aid in implementation of the plan. By personalizing the strategic plan through the executive summary, the CEO creates an excellent vehicle for follow-up communication and implementation. There is a direct relationship between the CEO's views and the specific decisions and actions that need to be undertaken to implement the plan. The executive summary helps ensure that the CEO's views will be put into action by the total organization.

## What Does the Executive Summary Contain?

The executive summary, written by the CEO in narrative form after the other sections of the plan have been completed, is dated, personally signed, and usually no more than two or three pages in length. It should address at least the following questions:

1.  *How are you performing in relation to your previous strategic plan?* This question addresses the credibility issue (are you managing according to your plan?). This should be dealt with early in the executive summary. If no plan is in place, state the reasons why you have embarked on this planning effort.
2.  *What are the key financial projections for your organization over the planning period?* Answers to this question include sales history and projections as well as profit history and projections.
    In addressing this question, it is helpful to establish trends by presenting financial history for the same number of years as those designated in the planning-period projections. Charts, graphs, or tables may be used in the presentation of this information.
3.  *What are the critical strategic issues that will affect your organization's performance? Why?* Here the CEO summarizes the exact nature of the critical issues facing the organization. Various sections of the plan may be referenced.
4.  *Why is the strategy identified in the plan appropriate for your organization?* Response to this question develops the rationale for exactly why this strategy was selected and how it fits into the CEO's vision for the organization.
5.  *What are the key factors necessary for successful implementation of the plan?* The CEO is accountable for

implementation of the plan. The answer to this question summarizes the CEO's views on the key management challenges of plan implementation.

*Sample Executive Summary*

The following is adapted from an executive summary prepared by the president of an industrial products company that has embarked on strategic planning for the first time.

We have demonstrated our ability to perform operationally and to produce short-term results. The major challenge we now recognize is the need to bring an additional dimension to our business—that of strategic thinking and planning. Our markets must be more clearly defined. Our product specifications and applications, both present and future, must be more accurately defined and documented in relation to markets that are changing and will continue to change in the future. We need to be prepared, both as a management team and as an organization, to meet these challenges.

Because this represents our first formal strategic plan, let me outline the specific financial projections our management team has committed to as a result of going through the strategic planning process. Although these financial projections are ambitious, we feel they are realistic and attainable. However, achievement of these results is dependent on establishing a strategic direction and long-term focus, something we have not concentrated on in the past.

Our financial projections are as follows (sales and net income are in constant dollars):

|                          | 1987    | 1988    | 1989    |
|--------------------------|---------|---------|---------|
| Sales (millions)         | $20.4   | $22.4   | $24.5   |
| Net Income (millions)    | 2.4     | 3.0     | 3.5     |
| Return on Invested Capital | 18.4% | 19.5%   | 20.5%   |

The critical issue we face as a company is that our major product line is in a mature market. The high-growth markets of the 1960s and 1970s no longer exist for our current products. As a result, we spent a considerable amount of time and effort in this strategic planning process developing a long-term strategy that will guide us in developing new products and assist us in concentrating on specific market segments that will help us meet our financial projections. Our growth during the last three years has averaged only 4.5 percent per year. This has barely kept up with the rate of inflation. Our board of directors has not been satisfied with either our growth or our return on invested capital. Historically, our company has grown at rates of 8 to 10 percent per year, and our return on invested capital (ROIC) has been in the 15 to 20 percent range. However, during the past three years our ROIC has averaged 14 percent.

To achieve the results outlined above, we need to refocus our efforts on a new long-term direction. The strategy we have selected is to become a products-driven organization. That is, we need to expand and fill in the gaps in our current product line using our traditional manufacturing and engineering capabilities and strengths. In the past, our new-product focus has been fragmented, and the results have been unsatisfactory. Based on our results over the last three years, we have averaged less than 5 percent in new-product sales. We must significantly improve this trend. New-product sales should be in the range of 15 to 20 percent if we are to continue to grow this business in a steady and planned manner.

To implement this strategy, we must redirect our efforts away from our traditional view of the marketplace. Our marketing emphasis needs to give us a different way of looking at our opportunities. We need to better understand the problems and challenges of our customers. We need to examine new product applications and new market opportunities. This will require an introduction of new products with a precision that has not been previously demonstrated by this organization.

Let me address in a personal way my views on implementation of our strategic plan. In my judgment, our future as an organization will be dependent on our ability to carry through on this strategic plan. We are at a crossroad in our twenty-year history. As your president, I will do all in my power to provide the leadership, the direction, and the management expertise needed to grow the organization in a planned and profitable manner. One of the principal reasons we decided to embark on this strategic planning effort was to make planning a way of life, a way of thinking, throughout our organization.

My job as president is to achieve certain planned results. Every individual in our organization also needs to achieve certain planned results. If we are to make planning work, we need to pull together as a team. This strategic plan is only a starting point. We need the active involvement of everyone in the organization to achieve our true potential and successfully meet our long-term objectives.

The challenge I see before us is for every one of you in the organization to understand our mission statement and our business strategy. With that understanding, you must relate your job, your decisions, your actions, and your results to the needs of the business. Then, as you attain both your business and personal objectives, the company will attain its objectives.

John B. Smith
President
April 22, 1986

## What Are the CEO's Concerns in Writing the Executive Summary?

Three major concerns that many CEOs experience in writing their executive summary are the time it takes, confidentiality, and personal vulnerability.

Concern about time is a common problem among CEOs. The executive summary is not written in one sitting. It should be in a narrative format, even though that generally requires more time than an outline format. When a series of one-line statements is used, too much is left to individual interpretation.

The executive summary is also too important to be a mere duplication of the whole plan or of specific sections of it. The executive summary enables the CEO (or equivalent) to step back from the various sections of the strategic plan and put the management challenges and opportunities of the plan in perspective. Rather than being a repetition of the key points in the plan, it adds a new dimension to it. It is the CEO's personal viewpoint of what the plan means to the total organization. The time invested in writing the executive summary pays rich dividends to the CEO and to the organization.

The question of who will have access to the executive summary is another concern for many CEOs. Because the executive summary may contain sensitive information of strategic and competitive importance, many CEOs are concerned about confidentiality. However, by itself, the executive summary rarely provides sufficient detail to be of value to the competition. The CEO needs to be straightforward and candid about the unique challenges and opportunities facing the organization without being overly concerned about who else may see the document.

The possibility of becoming personally vulnerable because of what is written in the executive summary is another concern faced by some CEOs. The CEO's personal views or convictions about the future of the organization need to be expressed in a manner that is motivational. They must be imaginative, far-reaching, thought-provoking, and people oriented. This may entail some personal risk to the CEO, but the potential payoff is worth that risk. To get the team and the rest of the organization more involved in, and committed to, the strategic plan, the CEO must personalize the executive summary. This approach enables key managers to better understand the challenges facing the CEO.

## What Are the Additional Uses of the Executive Summary?

The CEO is the chief communicator for the organization. It is imperative for the CEO to generate, in external as well as internal stakeholders, an awareness of the strategic direction and needs of the organization. Stakeholders are defined as those groups who have a vested interest, or stake, in the success of the organization.

Those external groups to whom the CEO feels responsible or accountable may include: the board of directors, shareholders, the parent company, customers, suppliers, others in the industry, financial institutions, the investment community, union leadership, governmental agencies, and the local community. The executive summary provides an excellent foundation for the important and time-consuming task of ongoing communication and discussion with these external stakeholders. Although it may be impractical to share the entire strategic plan with all of these groups, portions of the executive summary can be extracted or expanded upon, depending on the needs of the particular group addressed.

The board of directors is normally the primary external stakeholder. The CEO is directly accountable to the board of directors for organizational results. Although the entire plan is shared with the board, the executive summary is the document that is reviewed and discussed in depth. The board involves itself at the level of the executive summary, not necessarily in the details of the entire plan. Its primary role is to understand, comment on, and endorse the executive summary specifically and the strategic plan generally. Based on this level of involvement, the CEO should be confident of the board's backing and support.

In addition, the executive summary becomes the focal point for communicating with various groups of internal stakeholders. Middle managers, first-line supervisors, engineers, production workers, sales people, and accountants all need to see the implications of the strategic plan from a global perspective as well as in relation to its impact in their own areas of responsibility.

Through frank communication with both internal and external stakeholders, the CEO increases their awareness and understanding of exactly what is needed to support the plan. At the same time, the stakeholder groups gain a clearer understanding of the benefits to them that will result from implementation of the plan.

## In Summary

The executive summary provides an overview of the entire strategic plan from the CEO's perspective. It highlights those specific sections of the plan that reflect the CEO's primary concerns and offers a personalized view of where the organization should be going. Although it is the last section of the strategic plan to be completed, it becomes the first part of the plan document. Chapter Ten provides a blueprint for strategic plan development and implementation, including when and how the plan should be communicated to others.

# 10

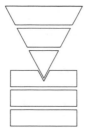

Developing
and Implementing
Your Strategic
Plan

Now that we have examined each of the elements of a strategic plan and the various factors that make up each element, it is time to bring them all together in a cohesive plan for development and implementation. Although each organization's specific requirements will be unique to its own situation, there are some fundamental implementation steps and special considerations that will put the process in perspective.

Strategic plan development refers to the actual building or creation of the strategic plan. It also includes the documentation of the plan.

Strategic plan implementation has two distinct components. One refers to the way in which the strategic plan is developed and communicated. This component will be addressed at the end of this chapter. The second component has to do with how the strategic plan is converted into operational plans and fully implemented throughout the organization. For example, how are the long-term objectives and integrated programs that are developed as part of the strategic plan actually translated into specific, measurable goals and action plans by all key managers and employees in the organization? This component is dependent on the successful undertaking of the strategic planning process in the first place, and then the carefully planned communication of this plan throughout the organization. This component of strategic plan implementation, the operational plan, will be addressed in the second book of this series.

### Are You Ready for Strategic Planning?

This is not a facetious question. The process of strategic planning may be reduced to that of just another paperwork exercise unless it is launched with a clear understanding on the part of those involved concerning:

- the amount of time required
- the number and type of meetings
- the individual preparation effort
- the various roles of the team members
- the mind set of participants
- and other similar issues

Strategic planning should not be entered into lightly. It requires considerable time and concentration from the members of the planning team. Furthermore, if the team's attention is focused primarily on current profit concerns, restructuring, or other operational problems, it may make sense to postpone the strategic planning effort until team members can devote more attention to a longer term view.

The following questions, addressed by the planning team members individually and then as a group, may help determine the degree of readiness:

1. Why do we want to undertake a strategic plan at this time? Is it a top priority?
2. What do we expect the strategic plan to do for us? How realistic is this?
3. In prior strategic planning efforts, what went well? What didn't go well? What do we need to do differently this time?

4. Do we have the necessary resources, knowledge, skill, and attitudes to successfully develop a strategic plan within the desired time frame?

Team members need to reach a consensus in their answers to these questions before moving ahead. Like other management processes, strategic planning must be organized, communicated, and implemented systematically.

The planning assessment checklist presented in Figure 10.1 is a tool that can both test the readiness of the organization for planning and quickly evaluate the effectiveness and completeness of current planning practices. This can be used by the CEO alone or as a discussion stimulator with the planning team. We recommend going through the checklist, placing a check in the appropriate column for each item. "O.K." means your current planning process addresses that item satisfactorily. "Need" indicates either that that item should be added or that a more effective application is required. "N/A" represents an item that is not applicable to your situation. After completing the initial checks, review each of the items with a mark in the "Need" column and determine what action is required, by when and by whom. Figure 10.2 is an example of a checklist completed by a CEO.

## What Is a Plan to Plan, and How Is It Created?

Although many executives will acknowledge the need for planning and will make every effort to do a thorough job of it, a relatively simple step that is frequently overlooked is the establishment of a plan to plan. This is not just a play on words. It clearly identifies that there are significant steps in the planning process that need to be completed if planning is to be an effective management tool. Therefore, we recommend that every organization design and establish its own plan to plan. What this does is identify what specific portions of the planning process need to be developed, fix a schedule for completion of each of these steps, and then establish a record of performance

## Figure 10.1. Planning Assessment Checklist.

| | CURRENT STATUS | | | ACTION (When & Whom) |
|---|---|---|---|---|
| | O.K. | NEED | N/A | |
| Integrated Planning Process understood | | | | |
| Plan to plan | | | | |
| Planning roles clarified | | | | |
| - CEO | | | | |
| - Senior executive team | | | | |
| - Board | | | | |
| - Coach/facilitator | | | | |
| - Planning coordinator | | | | |
| - Internal planning staff | | | | |
| - Other managers | | | | |
| Other employees | | | | |
| Planning team selected | | | | |
| | | | | |
| STRATEGIC PLANNING | | | | |
| Organization mission | | | | |
| Strategic analysis | | | | |
| - External opportunities & threats | | | | |
| - Market segments | | | | |
| - Industry & competition | | | | |
| - Technology | | | | |
| - Internal strengths & limitations | | | | |
| - Financial | | | | |
| - Products/services | | | | |
| - Internal capabilities | | | | |
| - Analysis assignments | | | | |
| - Critical issues | | | | |
| - Major conclusions | | | | |
| Strategy statement | | | | |
| Long-term objectives | | | | |
| Integrated programs | | | | |
| Financial projections | | | | |
| Executive summary | | | | |
| Strategic plan implementation | | | | |

*Source: The Executive Guide to Strategic Planning* by Patrick J. Below, George L. Morrisey, and Betty L. Acomb. San Francisco: Jossey-Bass. Coypright © 1987. Permission to reproduce hereby granted.

**Figure 10.2. Example of a Completed Planning Assessment Checklist.**

| | CURRENT STATUS | | | ACTION (When & Whom) |
|---|---|---|---|---|
| | O.K. | NEED | N/A | |
| Integrated Planning Process understood | ✓ | | | *update and reinforce* |
| Plan to plan | | ✓ | | *draft by 2/1 – Doris* |
| Planning roles clarified | | | | |
|   – CEO | ✓ | | | |
|   – Senior executive team | ✓ | | | |
|   – Board | | ✓ | | *I will handle – next mtg.* |
|   – Coach/facilitator | | ✓ | | *candidates identified 2/1 – Sam* |
|   – Planning coordinator | ✓ | | | |
|   – Internal planning staff | | | ✓ | |
|   – Other managers | | | ✓ | |
|   – Other employees | | | ✓ | |
| Planning team selected | ✓ | | | |
| | | | | |
| STRATEGIC PLANNING | | | | |
| Organization mission | ✓ | | | |
| Strategic analysis | | | | |
|   – External opportunities & threats | | ✓ | | *I will prepare by 2/1* |
|     – Market segments | ✓ | | | *let's discuss – staff mtg. – Bill* |
|     – Industry & competition | ✓ | | | |
|     – Technology | ✓ | | | |
|   – Internal strengths & limitations | | ✓ | | *I will prepare by 2/1* |
|     – Financial | ✓ | | | |
|     – Products/services | ✓ | | | |
|     – Internal capabilities | | ✓ | | *assessment by 2/1 – Sam* |
|   – Analysis assignments | ✓ | | | |
|   – Critical issues | ✓ | | | |
|   – Major conclusions | ✓ | | | |
| Strategy statement | | ✓ | | *reclarify – 2/21 planning mtg.* |
| Long-term objectives | ✓ | | | |
| Integrated programs | | ✓ | | *see plan to plan* |
| Financial projections | ✓ | | | |
| Executive summary | | ✓ | | *I will prepare by 4/15* |
| Strategic plan implementation | | ✓ | | *plan developed by 5/1 – Sam* |

against that schedule. This, as was mentioned earlier, is frequently one of the principal responsibilities of the planning coordinator.

Figure 10.3 is a sample plan to plan for a company. For such a plan to be useful, each organization needs to develop its own, based on its specific planning requirements. Typically, the final event in the plan to plan will be review and approval by whoever has the final say. Usually there is a specific time frame within which approval must take place. The approval may be by a board of directors, a parent company, some other higher-level body, or by the CEO and the planning team themselves. At any rate, by establishing a specific deadline by which approval must be obtained, it is possible to work backward and determine a realistic schedule for completion of each of the strategic plan elements. Obviously, the amount of time required for each of these steps will vary considerably depending on the nature of the business, the complexities to be addressed, and the degree to which portions of the planning process (for example, the organization's mission statement) have been satisfactorily completed in prior years.

An annual planning calendar is a very effective method that many organizations use in creating their plan to plan. The purpose of this calendar is to outline for the entire year the meetings required for strategic planning, operational planning, and results management. Such a calendar goes a long way toward ensuring that planning is an ongoing priority, and that planning or review meetings are scheduled far enough in advance to avoid schedule conflicts.

Our experience has shown that failure to establish a clear plan to plan that is readily understood by all who must contribute to the strategic plan will inevitably result in a plan that is substantially less effective.

## Who Is Selected for the Planning Team?

Strategic planning is primarily a senior management responsibility. The group that typically comprises the plan-

Figure 10.3. Sample Plan to Plan.

Strategic Planning Process
Plan to Plan

*Objective:*     To complete the update of our strategic plan by May
             15, 19____.

| Action Steps | Timetable |
|---|---|
| 1.  Preplanning meeting | January 15 |
| 2.  Two-day planning meeting | February 1–2 |
| • Overview of process | |
| • Organization mission review | |
| • Critical issues identification | |
| • Situation analysis assignments | |
| 3.  Undertake analysis assignments | February 3–28 |
| 4.  Two-day planning meeting | March 1–2 |
| • Review of analysis assignments | |
| • Strategy evaluation | |
| • Long-term objectives | |
| 5.  Two-day planning meeting | April 1–2 |
| • Finalization of strategy statement | |
| • Integrated programs | |
| 6.  Document strategic plan | April 15–30 |
| 7.  One-day planning meeting | May 15 |
| • Presentation, review, and approval of strategic plan (including financial projections and executive summary) | |

ning team is the CEO and those who report directly to
the CEO. However, there may be exceptions, such as an industry expert, a board member, key staff people, or certain middle managers who may provide valuable contributions to the planning effort. The team is selected to provide the best possible thinking and expertise available to
chart the long-term future of the organization. You may
wish to review the various planning responsibilities discussed in Chapter Two (pp. 21–25).

The size of the team is usually between five and ten
individuals. More than ten participants is cumbersome.
When additional persons or skills are needed, appropriate
individuals may be invited to participate in specific phases
of the process. The timely management of the process
toward a cohesive plan is a desired result.

## How Much Time Is Required?

Strategic planning, if it is to be productive, requires a significant investment of executive time. This is why we suggest reviewing your readiness before beginning your strategic planning process. Although there will be significant differences based on the organization and complexity of a particular plan, each planning team member should be prepared to invest between seven and twelve days over a three- to six-month period. This includes reading and other initial preparation, participation in four to eight team meetings, and individual assignments. A planning team making its first attempt should anticipate the longer span.

The estimated number of meeting days required to cover each of the elements of a strategic plan can be seen in Table 10.1. See Table 10.2 for what is appropriately covered in each of four team meetings and Table 10.3 for how the plan elements might be addressed in a series of eight meetings. You need to design a meeting plan that will work best for your team. Specific assignments, particularly in strategic analysis, need to be completed by individual

Table 10.1. Time Required for Strategic Planning.

| Elements of Strategic Plan | Team Meeting Time (Days) | |
|---|---|---|
| | Minimum | Maximum |
| Introduction to process | ½ | 1 |
| Organization mission | ½ | 1 |
| Strategic analysis | 2 | 3 |
| Strategy formulation | ½ | 1 |
| Long-term objectives | ½ | 1 |
| Integrated programs | 1 | 2 |
| Financial projections Executive summary Review of plan | 1 | 1 |
| Total days | 6 | 10 |

Table 10.2. Elements Addressed During Four Team Meetings.

| Elements of Strategic Plan | Team Meetings 1 | 2 | 3 | 4 |
|---|---|---|---|---|
| Introduction to process | X | | | |
| Organization mission | X | | | |
| Strategic analysis | X | X | | |
| Strategy formulation | X | X | | |
| Long-term objectives | | X | X | |
| Integrated programs | | | X | X |
| Financial projections | | | X | X |
| Executive summary | | | | X |
| Review of plan | | | | X |

Note: X indicates element(s) covered at each meeting.

Table 10.3. Elements Addressed During Eight Team Meetings.

| Elements of Strategic Plan | Team Meetings 1 | 2 | 3 | 4 | 5 | 6 | 7 | 8 |
|---|---|---|---|---|---|---|---|---|
| Introduction to process | X | | | | | | | |
| Organization mission | X | X | | | | | | |
| Strategic analysis | | X | X | X | | | | |
| Strategy formulation | | | | X | X | | | |
| Long-term objectives | | | | | X | X | | |
| Integrated programs | | | | | | X | X | |
| Financial projections | | | | | | | X | X |
| Executive summary | | | | | | | | X |
| Review of plan | | | | | | | | X |

Note: X indicates element(s) covered at each meeting.

team members between meetings. Typically such assignments may require the equivalent of one to two days of effort on the part of each member involved.

Although effective development of a strategic plan will consume a significant amount of executive time, it is important that the process not be dragged out indefinitely. Setting a schedule, as in the plan to plan, and staying with that schedule is one of the most effective ways of avoiding that problem. Even though you may not be completely satisfied with what you have developed, you are better off documenting and implementing a plan that is reasonably acceptable, with the understanding that you can modify or update it periodically (at least once a year).

One word of caution: Be wary of approaches that suggest a complete plan can be produced in one or two meetings. It is impossible to develop a viable strategic plan in one weekend or even in one week of concentrated effort. There is a distinctly different thought process and method of completion for each element. Also, time is required for the completion of individual assignments. Each element is developed independently and then checked with the others for consistency. Furthermore, spreading out the meetings allows time for the team to become comfortable with both the process and the plan itself.

## Who Leads the Planning Meetings?

Although the CEO provides the leadership for the total planning process, it is highly desirable that these team meetings be guided by an experienced planning coach/ facilitator. This role must be carefully defined, and the right person selected to fulfill it. Preferably, it should not be filled by someone from the executive team, even though some member or members may have the necessary skills. Each member of the team, including the CEO, must be free to express a personal view and take a strong position on certain issues. It is virtually impossible to do that and guide the process to its most productive conclusion at the same time.

The role of the coach/facilitator is primarily one of process more than content. This is an important distinction in this whole approach to strategic planning. We said at the outset of this book that the process of planning is as important as the product (that is, the plan document). This cannot, and should not, be overlooked by any organization that wants to strengthen or improve its planning process.

The process by which planning is carried out needs to promote open communication, trust, understanding, and belief. All of these are important ingredients in the whole people dimension of planning. As stated before, people, not plans, produce results. So the people dimension of planning needs to be carefully structured and managed. This is what is meant by *process.*

On the other hand, the content of the plan is equally important. There must be a good, solid strategic planning framework and information base from which decisions and judgments can be made. This includes a factual understanding of dynamics in the industry, competitive environment, and technology trends. The building of a strategic analysis data base is a key ingredient in the successful undertaking of your strategic planning effort.

However, expertise in the industry is not necessarily a major requirement of your coach/facilitator. That knowledge generally exists within the team or can be obtained as needed. The coach/facilitator assists and counsels the team, both as a group and individually, in the concepts, techniques, and methods of strategic planning. Guiding the process, assuring the airing of all relevant points of view, and when appropriate, confronting and challenging individual members of the team requires someone who is likely to be more objective.

**What Does a Strategic Plan Look Like?**

Each strategic plan is unique. It is designed around the organization's issues, needs, and opportunities. However, all strategic plans should contain each of the seven elements discussed earlier.

A sample table of contents from a plan for a $20 million company with 120 employees is shown in Figure

10.4. A typical plan will contain between twenty and forty pages. Essential backup data or additional detailed analysis may be included in a separate exhibit section of the plan, if needed. Strategic plans are not lengthy documents. They are designed to communicate the organization's future direction and to provide a broad road map for getting there.

**Figure 10.4. Sample Table of Contents for a Strategic Plan.**

| *Section* | *Page No.* |
|---|---|
| Executive Summary | 1–3 |
| Actual Dollars: Past Five Years | |
| Constant Dollars: Projected Five Years | |
| Organization Mission | 4 |
| Strategic Analysis | 5–15 |
| Markets/Products Analysis | |
| Bookings Review/Forecast | |
| Materials Cost | |
| Information Systems | |
| Human Resources | |
| Facilities | |
| Strategy Statement | 16 |
| Long-Term Objectives | 17 |
| Integrated Programs | 18–22 |
| Existing Sales Volume | |
| Materials Cost | |
| New Products—New and Existing Markets | |
| Financial Projections | 23–26 |
| The Integrated Planning Process | 27–28 |
| Strategic Plan Implementation | 29 |

## How Is the Plan Presented for Review and Approval?

The final step in plan development is review and approval of the plan by the board of directors, higher-level corporate management, a legislative body, or an internal management group that has approval authority. Many hours of effort have been invested by the team. It is important that their best story be presented. There are three major steps, with interim reviews as needed:

1.  *Draft review and preparation of the final document* provides one final opportunity for the team to review what has been developed to be certain it contains the specific message needed. It then can be modified before being reproduced in final form.
2.  *The package* must be reviewed to be certain it reflects the quality and importance of the document it contains. It does not need to be lavish, but it must look professionally prepared and should be bound in an attractive cover. It should be sent to the approving group for review in advance of the presentation.
3.  *The presentation* should be well rehearsed by those who will be verbally presenting the plan for approval. The presentation should highlight critical parts of the plan, including any interesting background data; it should not be a literal reading of the document. It is important to identify in the plan those crucial points where questions or comments from members of the approving group might be anticipated or encouraged. Other members of the team may act as members of the approval group during rehearsal periods, asking questions or offering comments that might be likely to come up during the actual presentation. The use of a video or audio tape recorder during rehearsal could help provide the feedback necessary to put polish on the presentation.

## How Is the Plan Communicated Throughout the Organization?

You must decide when and how others in the organization should get involved in the strategic planning process. This could take place while the plan is being developed or after the plan has been completed and approved.

Involving additional levels of management in the process while the plan is being developed makes sense when the organization is relatively small and close-knit. It increases the potential of ownership of the plan by others and provides an opportunity for critical input from additional key people whose ideas may be especially useful in determining the plan's content. This could include developing unit-level strategic plans or portions of plans (such as unit roles and missions), completing specific analysis assignments, and reviewing and making recommendations on sections of the plan while it is still in draft form. Disadvantages of involving others outside the planning team include an additional commitment of time on the part of those involved, a probable longer time span required for plan completion, and the potential of raising expectations or anxieties prematurely.

After the plan has been completed and approved, there are two basic approaches (with a number of variations) for involving additional levels; these are plan communication and unit-plan development. Plan communication has as its primary purpose familiarization of all key people in the organization with the plan so they can support it in their ongoing efforts. Unit-plan development involves creation of strategic plans at the unit level.

*Plan communication,* an informational sharing of the plan throughout the organization, is absolutely essential if the plan is to be implemented. This may seem obvious, but we find many organizations in which middle-level managers, let alone first-line supervisors and individual employees, are not aware of where the organization is going or why. Sharing information about the plan can and should be tremendously motivational because it gives others an opportunity to see where they fit in the total picture. This sharing should be done as soon as possible after plan approval so that momentum can be sustained. The method of sharing could range from distributing copies of the executive summary to a series of formal small-group presentations similar to that given to the approving group. Whenever possible, the CEO should be personally involved in these presentations and should be available to answer questions. In highly decentralized organizations where an actual visit by the CEO may not be practical, a videotape or closed circuit television presentation can be used instead.

*Unit-plan development* could be implemented uni-
formly throughout the organization. However, a selective
implementation plan based on the nature of the department's, or unit's, work and the readiness of the people
within that unit for strategic planning is probably more
realistic. There are certain functions, marketing or research
and development, for example, that tend to be more future oriented, and for them a complete strategic plan,
using the seven elements on a smaller scale, may be appropriate. In other areas, provision of unit roles and missions,
long-term objectives, and integrated programs may be all
that is needed. In still others, it may be sufficient simply
to tie in their short-term operational plans with the total
organizational plan.

If unit-plan development is being introduced for the
first time, we recommend spreading the full implementation effort over a two-year period, concentrating on unit
roles and missions as an initial step. In that way, you can
get started with the process without investing an excessive
amount of managerial time. Regardless of the approach
used, information about the plan needs to be communicated throughout the organization as comprehensively as
possible.

**In Summary**

The development and communication of a strategic
plan is the first of three major components in the Integrated Planning Process (see Figure 10.5). The strategic

Figure 10.5. Integrated Planning Process.

plan establishes the nature and future direction of the organization. To ensure effective implementation of the plan, the active involvement of the CEO and the planning team is required in each of its seven elements (see Figure 10.6). Then the organization is ready to move ahead into

Figure 10.6. Strategic Plan Framework.

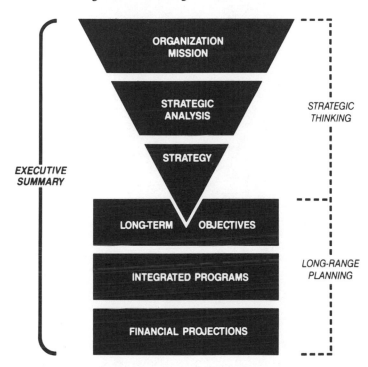

the operational plan and then into corporate performance and control (results management), which will be addressed in the next two volumes in this series.

The key to success in the Integrated Planning Process lies in getting the involvement and commitment of everyone in the organization. Remember, the purpose of planning is not to produce plans; it is to produce results, and this requires total organization commitment.

# Further Resources:
# Strategic Analysis
# Techniques

The purpose of this Appendix is to outline briefly some practical strategic analysis techniques. These techniques may be useful in helping to structure and present the analysis assignments outlined in Chapter Four. One value of these techniques is their usefulness in portraying complex situations or issues in a very visible manner. Another advantage of their use may be that of structuring a situation in a unique way that has strategic impact. For example, the life-cycle method of analysis enables executives to step back and ask the question: Where are we in terms of the overall life cycle of this particular factor? (The factor may be a product line, a market segment, an organization, an industry, or a technology.) By stepping back and taking a broad perspective of the situation, new insights or new and creative ways of looking at issues are often developed.

Remember, these analysis techniques are just that. They are techniques, not substitutes for good, solid executive judgment. A strategic plan, including a decision to pursue a particular strategy, should not be based solely on what is revealed through the use of one particular analytical technique. Where possible, more than one technique should be used to cross-check both the analysis being made and the conclusions suggested. Furthermore, both quantitative and qualitative information should be used in applying these various techniques. This approach helps balance facts with intuition and judgment.

These techniques should be used in a selective manner. If they fit a particular situation or analysis, they should be applied. However, do not try to force use of a particular analysis technique if it doesn't enhance the analysis.

The specific strategic analysis techniques described here include gap analysis, the product-market matrix, portfolio analysis, and the life-cycle concept.

These strategic analysis techniques provide concise, effective methods for analyzing and portraying major trends, major factors to be considered, strategic insights, and the like involved in the analysis and decision-making process. There are other approaches described in the literature that are worthy of consideration also. These techniques, when appropriately applied, lend credibility and preciseness to strategic analysis. Don't underestimate their simplicity. They are powerful ways of depicting complex situations in a very practical yet comprehensive manner.

## A. GAP ANALYSIS

The gap analysis technique is a simple but effective method of strategic analysis. The purpose of this technique is first to determine whether a gap exists in a particular situation and then, if one does, to describe what is needed to fill it. Figure A.1 portrays this technique.

Figure A.1. Gap Analysis.

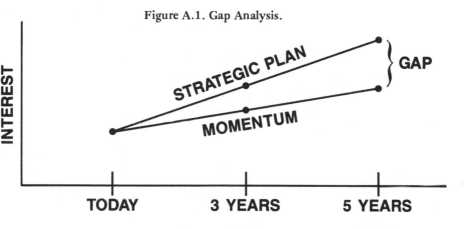

The approach for using the gap analysis technique is as follows:

1.  Identify the main interest in terms of strategic planning factors. This may be sales projections, net profit, return on investment, or whatever else is relevant.
2.  Identify current momentum or where current projections are likely to take you in the future (generally within three to five years).
3.  Identify the specific objectives you would like to accomplish via the strategic plan.
4.  Identify the difference between the strategic plan objectives and the current momentum. This is the gap that needs to be filled.
5.  Finally, identify specific programs, results, and actions required to fill the gap.

Another effective use of gap analysis is in reconciling top-down planning expectations and bottom-up projections. For example, if the CEO is looking for a 20 percent return on investment and analysis shows that 16 percent is more realistic, there needs to be either a discussion and resolution of means for filling this 4 percent gap or a revision of the top-down requirements.

# B. PRODUCT-MARKET MATRIX

The purpose of this technique, highlighted by George Steiner (1977) and others, is to depict, in a matrix format, the relationship between major product/service lines and various market segments. This approach is illustrated in Figure B.1.

Figure B.1. Product-Market Matrix: Application A.

| PRODUCT/SERVICE LINES | MARKET SEGMENTS | |
| --- | --- | --- |
| | PRESENT | FUTURE |
| PRESENT | | |
| FUTURE | | |

The product-market matrix requires identification of and agreement on both present and future product and/or service lines. Identification of and agreement on present and future market segments is also required. The matrix may be completed using such information as total sales in dollars, unit sales, percentages of product mix, profitability, percentages of market share, and market growth trends. The result of this approach is the portrayal of the product/

service and market relationships that are of strategic importance to the organization. For example, future growth or expansion of a product line coupled with a corresponding growth in a related market segment would suggest a strong strategic opportunity.

Another application of the product-market matrix is shown in Figure B.2. This matrix may be used to identify

Figure B.2. Product-Market Matrix: Application B.

| MARKET \ PRODUCT | PRESENT | RELATED | UNRELATED |
|---|---|---|---|
| PRESENT | LOW RISK → | | HIGH RISK |
| RELATED | | | |
| UNRELATED | HIGH RISK | | EXCESSIVE RISK |

Source: Steiner, 1977, p. 18. Used by permission.

the potential risk involved as future products and markets are compared. The position in the matrix is strategically significant as plans are developed.

# C. PORTFOLIO ANALYSIS

Portfolio analysis, illustrated in Figure C.1, is market-segment oriented as the company's market share and the growth rate of the market are compared.

Figure C.1. Portfolio Analysis.

**GROWTH RATE**

| | | HI | LO |
|---|---|---|---|
| **MARKET SHARE** | **HI** | *GROWTH OPPORTUNITY* | *INCOME GENERATOR* |
| | **LO** | *UNCERTAIN?* | *DIVEST?* |

This matrix may be used to analyze individual business units, major product lines, or major market segments. By portraying them as shown in Figure C.1, strategic insights can be gathered and conclusions reached regarding potential business, product, and market directions. The Boston Consulting Group* has been credited with developing this four-box matrix.

## D. LIFE-CYCLE CONCEPT

The practical and creative approach known as the life-cycle concept is illustrated in Figure D.1.

Figure D.1. Life-Cycle Concept.

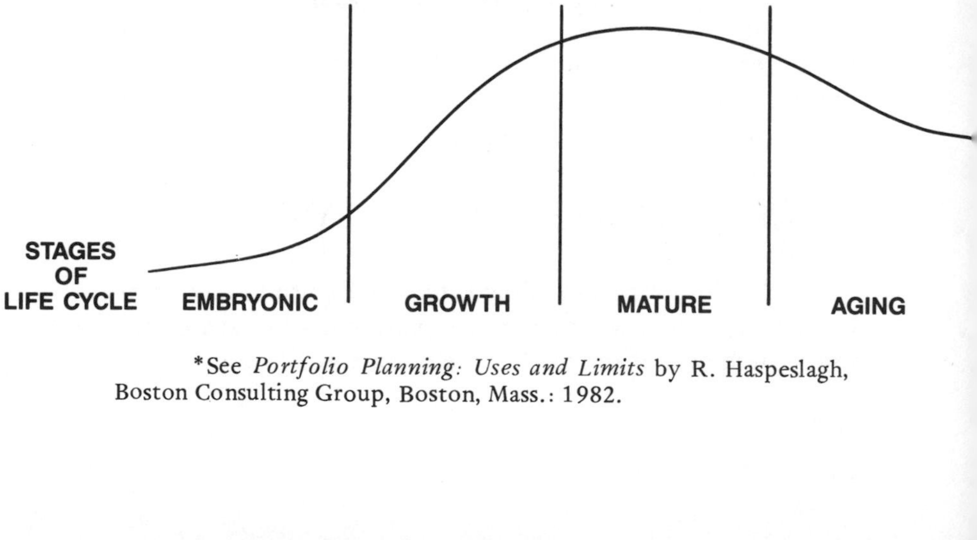

**STAGES OF LIFE CYCLE**    EMBRYONIC    GROWTH    MATURE    AGING

*See *Portfolio Planning: Uses and Limits* by R. Haspeslagh, Boston Consulting Group, Boston, Mass.: 1982.

The life-cycle concept may be applied to such factors as products, markets, technology, an industry, or an organization. By assessing where these factors are in their life-cycles, new perspectives can be gained in terms of present and future actions that are required or major conclusions to be reached about these particular areas.

# Annotated Bibliography

Of the many publications available in the field of strategic planning, we have selected a few we feel will be particularly useful to those who wish to study the field in more depth. They are annotated here.

Albert, Kenneth J. (editor in chief). *Handbook of Strategic Management.* New York: McGraw-Hill, 1983.
This publication includes twenty-five articles on the subject of strategic planning and strategic management by some of the best-known experts in the field. This is more than a book of readings, since many of the articles were prepared especially for this handbook. Its strength lies in the diversity of the many points of view it presents.

Brandt, Steven C. *Strategic Planning In Emerging Companies.* Reading, Mass.: Addison-Wesley, 1981.
Steven Brandt has specialized in entrepreneurship and managing practices for high-growth companies. This compact book provides some keen insights into the challenges facing managers in rapidly expanding companies. It includes some classic readings from major business periodicals.

Dible, Donald M. *Up Your OWN Organization.* (3rd ed.) Englewood Cliffs, N.J.: Prentice-Hall, 1986.

    This no-nonsense entrepreneur's guide is written by a man who has been there many times. It provides an inside out look at what is involved in true entrepreneurship, the various elements of a business plan and how to put them together, plus some practical approaches to gaining access to money sources. It is must reading for those in start-up ventures.

Drucker, Peter F. *Innovation and Entrepreneurship: Practice and Principles.* New York: Harper & Row, 1985.

    Peter Drucker, in his inimitable manner, provides an eye-opening view of the important differences between inventors and innovators, speculators and entrepreneurs. He has identified seven sources for innovation that need to be carefully considered by any organization desiring strategic movement.

Kastens, Merritt L. *Long-Range Planning for Your Business: An Operating Manual.* New York: AMACOM, 1976.

    This book, as the title implies, is a practical operating guide on how to do long-range planning. Its strength is in the straightforward manner used in describing how to do planning, not just talk about it. The book is particularly strong on the mechanics of long-range planning.

O'Connor, Rochelle. *Corporate Guides to Long-Range Planning,* Report no. 687. New York: Conference Board, 1976.

    This research report provides a detailed examination of the long-range planning documents, guidelines, and instructions used by a wide variety of corporations to help their managers produce long-range plans. A total of eighty-three company planners contributed to this study.

O'Connor, Rochelle. *Preparing Managers for Planning,* Report no. 781. New York: Conference Board, 1980.

    One hundred nine planning executives describe and appraise their firms' planning education activities in this first survey of the Conference Board's Panel of Planning Executives. This survey addressed how to prepare and educate managers for strategic planning.

O'Connor, Rochelle. *Facing Strategic Issues: New Planning Guides and Practices,* Report no. 867. New York: Conference Board, 1985.
This report updates report number 687, published in 1976. The planning practices of 214 companies are represented in this study. Of these, 115 submitted copies of company planning instructions, guides, and manuals from which exhibits were selected.

Odiorne, George S. *Strategic Management of Human Resources: A Portfolio Approach.* San Francisco: Jossey-Bass, 1984.
This book is especially helpful for those required to analyze human resources in the strategic planning process. George Odiorne shows how to apply portfolio analysis to human resource management and offers practical approaches for managing and capitalizing on high-performing employees.

Ohmae, Kenichi. *The Mind of the Strategist: The Art of Japanese Business.* New York: McGraw-Hill, 1982.
Known as Mr. Strategy in his native Japan, Kenichi Ohmae addresses the art of strategic thinking as a key ingredient in successful strategic planning. The focus is more on the substance of strategic planning than on the form. He also addresses the myths and realities of Japanese management, including what we in the United States can learn from Japan about the strategic planning process.

Porter, Michael E. *Cases in Competitive Strategy: Techniques for Analyzing Industries and Competitors.* New York: Free Press, 1980.
Porter, Michael E. *Competitive Advantage: Creating and*

*Sustaining Superior Performance.* New York: Free Press, 1985.

> These two books provide a wealth of information on approaches and techniques for competitive analysis. They are especially useful for market analysts required to come up with the data needed to complete market segment analyses in highly competitive industries.

Schaffir, Walter B. *Strategic Planning: Making It Work.* Paper presented at the Conference Board's Strategic Planning Conference, New York City, March 31, 1982.

> This brief, but very practical, monograph highlights the importance of two key aspects of strategic planning: the important role of the planning coach/facilitator and determining the truly critical long-term issues facing an organization.

Schein, Edgar H. *Process Consultation: Its Role in Organization Development.* Reading, Mass.: Addison-Wesley, 1969.

> This is not a book about planning. It is a book about process that is especially useful for those performing the coach/facilitator function. It is an early classic in the field.

Shaeffer, Ruth G. *Developing Strategic Leadership,* Report no. 847. New York: Conference Board, 1984.

> This research report was prepared to help U.S. companies share ideas and information on effective ways to develop strategic leadership within their organizations. Eighteen CEOs from a wide variety of businesses were interviewed concerning their views on this topic.

Steiner, George A. *Strategic Managerial Planning.* Oxford, Ohio: Planning Executives Institute, 1977.

> This brief booklet covers many of the key elements included in Steiner's *Strategic Planning: What Every Manager Must Know.* It provides a useful shopping list of planning approaches and techniques.

Steiner, George A. *Strategic Planning: What Every Manager Must Know.* New York: Free Press, 1979.
George Steiner's contributions to strategic and long-range planning are legend. This book provides a comprehensive approach to strategic planning, including a wide variety of analytical techniques. It is especially useful for those wanting an in-depth understanding of the strategic planning process.

Tregoe, Benjamin B., and Zimmerman, John W. *Top Management Strategy: What It Is and How to Make It Work.* New York: Simon & Schuster, 1980.
This clear, definitive work on the meaning and application of strategy in the planning process is must reading for anyone wishing to have a clearer focus on the future direction of their business.

# Index